S0-AEW-140

COOKING KOSHER THE NEW WAY

Fast, Lite & Natural

Cooking Kosher the New Way

Fast, Lite & Natural

Jane Kinderlehrer

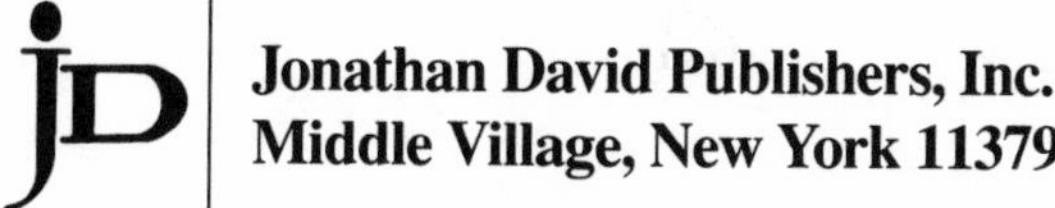
Jonathan David Publishers, Inc.
Middle Village, New York 11379

COOKING KOSHER THE NEW WAY

Copyright © 1995
by
Jane Kinderlehrer

No part of this book may be reproduced in any form without the prior written consent of the publishers. Address all inquires to:

Jonathan David Publishers, Inc.
68-22 Eliot Avenue
Middle Village, New York 11379

2 4 6 8 10 9 7 5 3

Library of Congress Cataloging-in-Publication Data
Kinderlehrer, Jane.
Cooking kosher the new way : fast, lite & natural/
by Jane Kinderlehrer.

p. cm.

Rev. ed. of: Cooking kosher, the natural way. 1980.
Includes index.

ISBN 0-8246-0380-X

1. Cookery, Jewish. 2. Quick and easy cookery. 3. Low-fat diet-Recipes. 4. Salt-free diet—Recipes. 5. Sugar-free diet—Recipes. 6. Cookery (Natural foods) I. Kinderlehrer, Jane. Cooking kosher, the natural way. II. Title.

TX724.K56 1995

641.5'676—dc20 95-6216

CIP

Book design by Marcy Stamper

Printed in the United States of America

To the girls in my cooking class—

for the joy we share as we

expand our culinary horizons

❧

CONTENTS

Foreword

Ever since the publication of my *Cooking Kosher the Natural Way,* I have been besieged with requests from all over this country and Israel for more recipes and more health information geared to the kosher cook who wants to provide health-building meals with a Yiddishe *tam* (taste) but who has little time to cook.

Let's face it, times have changed since Mama rose early in the morning and spent a long, long day baking challah and strudel, making pot roast and kishke, and tsimmes, knishes, and chopped liver.

The good news is that, with a big assist from modern conveniences like the blender, food processor, seed and nut grinder, and microwave oven, you can delight your family with the time-honored dishes Grandma spent hours preparing and make them in jig time.

Weight Control

When it comes to providing meals that foster good health and weight control, the microwave oven can be your friend and ally. That's because foods simmer in their own juices in the microwave or steam in their own vapor—so no extra fat is needed to keep them from sticking to the pot.

Convenience

You no longer have to decide in the morning what to make for dinner so you can get the ingredients out of the freezer to defrost by evening. Now, you can make last-minute decisions and defrost in minutes. This makes it possible to offer impromptu invitations.

The Joy of Leftovers

Leftovers are no longer a drag. They're a joy. Store them in individual portions, then label and freeze them. They make wonderful lunches and help-yourself breakfasts for the children.

Building Better Hearts, Bones, Brains, and Dispositions

Granted that, in this harried age, it's important to be able to prepare meals quickly. But, let's put first things first: to provide meals that contribute to better health is even more important.

There has been an explosion of new research in the health field that points to various foods as heart savers, bone-builders, or cancer preventives. How to incorporate these health-building nutrients into kosher meals that retain their connection with tradition is the challenge faced by today's homemaker, especially the working person whose interests range far beyond the kitchen.

With guidance from *Cooking Kosher the New Way,* you will learn how to cut the fat; how to make food tasty without salt; how to enjoy the sweet life without sugar or artificial sweeteners.

The recipes I have designed for you will not expand your waistline with empty calories; they won't clog your arteries with lots of fat; they are high in fiber, ridiculously low in fat, and they contain no sugar, white flour, hydrogenated fats, or chemical additives.

Moses Maimonides, the great Rambam, said, "No illness which can be treated by diet should be treated by any other means." Many of you agree. But so many of you have also lamented, "I'd love to cook naturally the way you do, but with a job and a houseful of kids I just don't have the time."

With your time-saving equipment and this book as your guide and inspiration, you will provide your loved ones with nutrients that prevent illness and promote a wonderful sense of well-being. Go to it!

Oh, yes! You'll be very happy to know that, while the recipes are all in accordance with holy writ, they taste sinfully good.

INTRODUCTION

Part I

Kosher Is Not Enough

Many of the special dishes from the wonderful world of kosher Jewish cookery have been handed down from mother to daughter for countless generations. In the process, they have picked up some ingredients which, in the light of the new knowledge of nutrition, are definite no-no's. They may be kosher, but they are neither wholesome nor nutritious. In fact, they have been shown to be harmful and have been implicated as contributing to such debilitating conditions as high blood pressure, diabetes, atherosclerosis, obesity, constipation, hyperactivity in children, pyorrhea, hemorrhoids, and other embarrassments one can live very nicely without.

Before going further, let's review what is meant by "kosher food." The word *kosher* literally means "fit or proper to be used." In Leviticus 11, the laws of *kashrut* (the kosher dietary laws) are set forth. Accordingly, those of us who observe the dietary laws are permitted to eat the following foods:

- all fruits and vegetables
- the meat on all animals that have split hooves and that chew the cud—beef, lamb, etc. Thus, pork or pork products are not permissible.
- all seafood that has fins and scales. Thus, foods such as shrimp, lobster, clams, and oysters are not permissible.
- most domesticated fowl, including chicken, duck, goose, pigeon, and squab.

In addition to being limited to certain foods, later (rabbinic) law added further requirements and restrictions. According to these laws, in order for meat to be kosher it has to be slaughtered by a shochet, an individual trained to slaughter animals with a razor-sharp knife in keeping with a specified procedure. Kosher meat that has been slaughtered in this manner is readily available today, not only in kosher butcher shops but in major supermarkets as well.

Rabbinic law also states that all meat or fowl must be *koshered* before it may be used. This procedure involves the rinsing and salting of the meat or fowl in order to remove the blood. Most meat sold commercially as kosher has already undergone this process, although it is possible to do this yourself at home.

One more important point: kosher law dictates that meat and dairy products not be mixed during cooking and serving. So, for example, chicken would not be basted with butter (a dairy product) during cooking, nor would butter be served at the same meal with chicken, even if the butter were intended to be used as a spread for rolls or bread.

Generally, we refer to meat products as being *fleishig* (sometimes pronounced *fleishik)* or *fleishedig (fleishedik)* and dairy products as *milchig (milchik)* or *milchedig (milchedik).* There are also foods that are neither fleishig nor milchig—including fruits and vegetables, grains, fish, eggs—and these are said to be *pareve.* Such "neutral" foods may be used in the preparation of a meat or dairy dish and may be served with a meat or dairy meal.

Centuries ago, the laws of kashrut protected those who observed them from many foods that proved to be troublemakers. Whether these laws were primarily designed for spiritual well-being is immaterial. The fact is that they have stood the test of time and, in fact, are still protecting us even though we now have advanced technology, refrigeration, and government inspection.

Some of the kosher dietary traditions may very well have served to prevent health hazards, particularly as regards to consumption of "unclean" animals, which are frequently fed leftover human food that is likely to be moldy. It is now recognized that some of the common molds can produce carcinogenic metabolites which behave like free radicals on a rampage.

So, the practice of eating kosher food has contributed much to the well-being of many people over the centuries. Though food is meant to be enjoyed, its first function is to nourish and sustain.

How To Add Nutrition to Tradition

Chopped liver with grated black radish, moistened with a whisper of rendered chicken fat and a bit of chopped onion—pure ecstasy! Fluffy knaidlach swimming in chicken soup; hot knishes, crisp and delicious with spicy potato, kasha, or cheese fillings; hamantaschen bursting with poppy seeds or prunes; or honey-soaked taiglach or creamy kugels—pure bliss to bite into. Mushroom and barley soup to warm your bones; hearty kasha varnishkes with hot gravy; strudel with heavenly fruit and nut fillings. You don't need a fiddler on the roof to tell you that these foods spell tradition. Their very names evoke blissful memories of small kibitzers crowding around the big black stove, and a lovely warm feeling that Mama's in the kitchen and all's right with the world.

One generation passes, another takes its place. Now, it's our turn. What kind of memories are we cooking up in our pots and pans? What kind of heavenly aromas say "Welcome home" to our families?

Can we, in this age of instant mashed potatoes, TV dinners, frozen overly sweet blintzes, nondairy creamers, and foam-rubber bread, provide not only the spirit and spice of Jewish hospitality, but also the nutrients we need for the lovely glow of health?

Sure we can!

- We can reduce the sugar and fat in kugels and make them kind to our arteries.
- We can provide delicious *nosherai* we'll be happy to see our families devour because every crumb contributes to health.
- We can provide delicious honey cakes, mandelbrodt, and strudel without sugar, without hydrogenated fats, and rich in health-building ingredients.
- We can serve delicious vegetarian meals several times a week and reduce our consumption of meat.

Cooking Kosher the New Way can help us give to our families both tradition and nutrition, the taste of love and an enduring link to our culinary roots.

Let's face it. Grandma's old favorites were high in sugar, salt, and hydrogenated fats.

This grandma, after extensive experimentation, has come up with adaptations of the old favorites, eliminated the negatives, added the positives, and multiplied our chances of enjoying them in good health. These are the recipes I shall hand down to my kitchen kibitzers and hopefully start a new tradition while preserving the *tam* of the old Jewish dishes.

The recipes that you will find in *Cooking Kosher the New Way* are in keeping with the spirit of the biblical injunction, "Take heed unto yourself and take care of your life" (Deuteronomy 4:9).

Part II
How to Naturalize Your Kitchen

If you were to ask me how to cook kosher the new way, I would say: *Stay as close to Nature as possible!* Cut down on fats and avoid the four whites: white sugar, white flour, refined white salt, and devitalized white rice. All the rest is commentary. Go thou and learn.

And there is much to learn. You start by discarding "negative foods" and stocking up on health-building foods. Caution: do it gradually.

In your good nutrition department, you should have:

1. WHEAT GERM, RAW OR TOASTED

Keep it refrigerated or in the freezer. Raw wheat germ has more nutrients than the toasted. The toasted has better keeping qualities and a flavor that is more acceptable to some palates. To give raw wheat germ a toasty flavor, toast about one-half cup in a 250-degree F. oven until light brown and add to the rest in the jar. The whole jar of wheat germ will taste toasted.

2. BRAN

Coarse miller's bran is available at health food stores and can be added, as a source of additional fiber, to cereals and baked goods. Be sure to increase liquids when you use bran. Like wheat germ, bran should be kept under refrigeration or frozen.

3. HONEY

Honey is twice as sweet as sugar, so you can use half as much to achieve the same level of sweetness. Honey's sweetness is derived from fructose, which, unlike sucrose, does not trigger an outpouring of insulin. Fructose is absorbed into the bloodstream at a much slower rate than sucrose, which makes it less likely to cause the "sugar blues."

Sugar provides only empty calories—no nutrients. Honey provides B vitamins and minerals like calcium, phosphorus, iron, and potassium and some important enzymes.Try to get raw, unprocessed, unfiltered honey. For the least processed honey, visit the "keeper of the bees." Next best is your natural foods store. If the honey in your jar has crystallized, rejoice! That's a sign that it has not been damaged by excessive heat. Just put the jar in warm water for a few minutes and the honey will liquefy.

When you are converting recipes that call for sugar, use ½ cup honey for every cup of sugar. Reduce the liquid in the recipe by ¼ cup for each ½ cup of honey substituted, and bake at a temperature 25 degrees lower than the instructions call for. If there is no liquid in the recipe, add ¼ cup more flour. (There is no need to make these adjustments for the recipes in this book.)

4. MOLASSES AND SUCANAT

Unsulphured molasses—preferably blackstrap. Use as a sweetener occasionally instead of honey, or use it half and half with honey until your family grows accustomed to the taste. It's a terrific source of iron and a good source of calcium, phosphorus, potassium, and the B vitamins. Put a teaspoon in a cup of hot water for a caffein-free "coffee" that gives you a lift and no letdown.

Sucanat, a natural whole-food sweetener fills the need for a dry sweetener while providing nutrients. Sucanat—evaporated sugar cane juice without additives and preservatives—provides all the vitamins, minerals, and nutrients of the sugar cane.

5. WHOLE-WHEAT FLOUR

Preferably stone ground. Keep it in the freezer or refrigerator and get it from a source where it is kept refrigerated. If no health food store or co-op in your area sells this top-quality flour, you can order it by mail from

Walnut Acres, Penn's Creek, Pennsylvania 17862. Their grains are stored in special cold rooms, thus obviating the necessity for the frequent fumigation to which commercial whole-grain flours are subjected. Since you are keeping your flour refrigerated, always warm it before combining it with yeast. Put as much as you need in the oven for fifteen minutes at 200 degrees F., or microwave it on medium for one minute.

6. SOY FLOUR

A protein booster and a cancer inhibitor. Two tablespoons added to one cup of flour will greatly enhance the protein and health value of your baked goods.

7. CAROB POWDER

Unlike cocoa and chocolate, carob (which has a chocolaty taste), has no theobromine (a caffeinlike substance), no oxalic acid which ties up calcium, no fat, very few calories and is rich in essential minerals. There is four times as much calcium in carob as there is in cocoa.

8. SEEDS

Sesame, sunflower, pumpkin, poppy, and flax seeds—all contain that mysterious vitality which can produce a new plant. Seeds are Nature's storehouse of enzymes, vitamins, minerals, protein, and essential fatty acids. Get them unsalted and unroasted. To enhance flavors, roast them yourself for ten minutes in a conventional oven at 250 degrees F. or for two minutes on medium in the microwave. Combine seeds, nuts, and raisins for a dish of *nosherai* that will keep your family and guests munching happily and healthfully.

9. LECITHIN GRANULES AND SOY GRITS

Lecithin is a natural emulsifier. It helps keep cholesterol circulating happily. Recent research indicates that lecithin (soy grits is a good source) increases by a factor of three the amount of cholesterol that can be dissolved in bile salts. Bile salts are the vehicle by which the body rids itself of excess cholesterol. M.I.T. scientists have determined that lecithin in the diet improves memory and can actually make one "smarter." It helps manufacture acetylcholine, which helps the brain transmit nerve signals. Lecithin is high in phosphorus, which indicates a need for more calcium. Sesame seeds, dry milk, and green leafy vegetables are good sources of calcium.

10. BEANS, BEANS, BEANS

All kinds. Most beans require presoaking. Exceptions are lentils, split peas, and mung beans. If you keep a tray of dry soybeans in water in your freezer, you will always have presoaked beans ready to bring a measure of cancer protection to your soup, stew, casserole, or cholent. Or, presoak beans overnight. Next morning, pour off the soak water (give it to your plants), spread the beans on a cookie sheet and freeze. When the beans are hard as marbles, transfer to a plastic bag. Keep them in the freezer and use as few or as many as your dish requires.

Because of their high protein content, soybeans may be served occasionally as a substitute for meat or eggs. Serve with a grain, like brown rice or bulgur, and you will have a biologically complete protein pattern.

I keep a variety of beans—soy, navy, pinto, lima, aduki, garbanzo, kidney—in separate containers in the freezer. Thus, my creative culinary urges are not stymied by a long soaking period.

11. GRAINS

Buckwheat (kasha), barley, brown rice, wild rice, oats, and millet (a terrific high-protein grain said to be the manna from Heaven that sustained the Israelites on their trek through the desert) are all good sources of nutrients and fiber.

12. ARROWROOT POWDER

This natural thickening agent, a source of protein and trace minerals, is derived from the roots of plants that pull minerals from the soil. It is a much more natural and nutritious food than cornstarch, which is highly processed.

13. BAKING POWDER

Use the kind that is aluminum- and preferably sodium-free, available at natural food stores, or make your own by combining ¼ teaspoon baking soda with ½ teaspoon cream of tartar to make the equivalent of 1 teaspoon of baking powder.

14. HEALTHY HEART BUTTER

Do not be tempted to substitute margarine for butter. There is no comparison in taste and, healthwise, you're much better off with butter. The process of hydrogenation converts the polyunsaturates in margarine to trans acids, which have been shown to be even more damaging to the arteries than saturated fats or cholesterol.

If the fear of saturated fats has caused you to deny yourself the pleasure of butter, use my Healthy Heart Butter *(see page 250)*, which lowers the saturates and increases the polyunsaturates.

15. WHAT ABOUT CHICKEN FAT?

Chicken fat, or *schmaltz*, has long been the traditional fat in the preparation of many *geshmache* (very tasty) dishes. In fact, the word schmaltz has become part of colloquial English: "Schmaltz it up," a director will tell his cast. "Give it some schmaltz," an editor will advise a reporter. What they mean is give it some pizzazz; give it some tam.

And that's exactly what chicken fat, used discreetly, does for many dishes—chopped liver, knishes, kasha varnishkes; for mashed potatoes instead of butter; spread on rye bread for a nosh, or spread on bread instead of mayonnaise for a scrumptious chicken sandwich.

I can almost hear you exclaiming in horror, "What about the cholesterol?" Well, I have news for you. Chicken fat is not saturated like other animal fats. The fat in chicken is largely monounsaturated, the kind that tends to *lower* harmful cholesterol levels.

What about turkey and duck? They are similar in composition and in levels of unsaturation, but differ in vitamin E levels. Chicken fat contains about five times more vitamin E than turkey fat, with duck somewhere in the middle. Since vitamin E is a powerful antioxidant which destroys disease-causing free radicals, and in the process prevents rancidity, chicken fat has a longer keeping period.

Part III

Do Your Heart a Favor: Cut the Fat and Savor the Flavor

There was a time, not so long ago, when a man who sported a "corporation" (ample midsection) and whose wife had a "proper double chin" was looked upon as successful, as living off the fat of the land. Times have changed.

Traditional Jewish cooking, with all its richness, is very high in fat and, tragically, we are suffering the consequences. Cardiovascular disease, diabetes, and cancer of the stomach and colon, all associated with a high-fat diet, are more prevalent among Jewish people than any other ethnic group.

What to do about it? Cut down on the fat and enjoy a longer, healthier, more productive life. Happily, you can accomplish this without sacrificing the *geshmache* flavor. Here are some healthful hints.

- You can make food brown and crispy without deep-frying. Lightly brush with olive or canola oil, or shpritz with nonstick cooking spray and broil about 8 inches from the oven element.
- Sauté in liquid. Instead of sautéing in oil, cook over high heat in a small amount of water, stock, wine, or tomato juice.
- Sauté thinly-sliced vegetables such as yellow squash, zucchini, peppers, and onions in two tablespoons of tomato juice. Toss with herbs such as oregano, basil, and thyme and serve as a side dish. Or, add cubed tofu to the sauté pan and serve as a high-protein main dish. Nice with a garnish of toasted sesame or sunflower seeds.
- Sauté chicken or fish in flavored vinegars.
- Sauté sliced vegetables together with mushrooms, which automatically release lots of liquid.
- Cook stew and soup the day before and refrigerate them overnight so the fat will rise to the top, where it can be easily skimmed off.
- Use a marinade or wine instead of fat to baste meat and poultry. In your marinades, use soup stock, herbal tea, or fruit juice instead of oil.

- In place of oil, use fresh lemon or lime on salads.
- If you do use salad dressing, reduce the fat by replacing at least two-thirds of the oil with puréed cucumber.
- Slim down the mayonnaise. There's a whopping 100 calories in one tablespoon. For dairy dishes you can cut the mayonnaise with low-fat yogurt, only 36 calories in four tablespoons.
- Instead of shmearing your bagel with full-fat cream cheese, use Neufchâtel, a soft dairy cheese with 25 percent fewer calories. Or even better, use cream cheese made from drained low-fat yogurt.
- Instead of decorating your special desserts with whipped cream, try this lowfat dessert topping: combine 1½ cups of plain lowfat yogurt with ¼ cup of nonfat dry milk, 2 tablespoons honey, ½ teaspoon grated lemon rind, ⅓ teaspoon freshly grated nutmeg, and a dash of ground ginger. Beat well or whiz in a food processor. Delicious on cooked fruit desserts, pies, cobblers, and cakes.
- Instead of using butter or sour cream on your baked potato, use lowfat yogurt spiked with chopped scallions or mashed tofu seasoned with an herb-and-spice blend.
- Many of us nosh on crackers, thinking they are low-calorie. Most are not. Some crackers contain large amounts of fat. Always check the ingredient list on the package. Avoid it if butter or oil is among the first three ingredients.
- Use yogurt as a thickener instead of part of the oil or cream. For salad dressing: to ¼ teaspoon Dijon mustard, 1 teaspoon herbal seasoning, and 2 tablespoons wine vinegar, add 1 tablespoon oil and 3 tablespoons yogurt.
- Cut the fat in peanut butter by combining it with an equal amount of mashed cooked carrots or mashed ripe banana.

Cooking Kosher the New Way

Fast, Lite & Natural

1

Wake Up Your Life (With a Lowfat High-Fiber Breakfast)

❧

If you are skipping breakfast in order to lose weight, STOP! You are defeating your purpose. You are keeping the motors of your metabolism in low gear. What you want to do, in order to burn calories, is shift into high. How do you do that? By putting high-octane nutrients, proteins, and complex carbohydrates in your tank. Such a breakfast stokes the fires of your metabolism, keeps your blood sugar on an even keel, and contributes to energy, clear thinking, and a sense of well-being.

Many studies have demonstrated that without breakfast or with one that is mostly sugar and starch, students show a poorer attitude toward schoolwork and adults become less efficient in the late-morning hours. If you or your children are so rushed in the morning that you don't have time to prepare and sit down to a good breakfast, try some of the following morning beverage combinations. They're ready in an instant and will keep you perking along energetically until noon.

ALL-PURPOSE DYNAMITE DRINK

Make this nutrient-rich mix ahead of time and your mornings will be hassle-free.

¼ cup sunflower seeds

¼ cup sesame seeds

¼ cup almonds

¼ cup rolled oats

¼ cup carob powder

¼ cup wheat germ

¼ cup oat bran

½ cup nonfat dry milk powder

In a blender, food processor, or seed mill, grind the seeds, nuts, and oats very fine. Add the carob powder, wheat germ, oat bran, and dry milk powder and mix thoroughly. Store in a glass jar in the refrigerator or freezer.

To serve, use ¼ cup dry mix to 1 cup of liquid (lowfat milk, water, or fruit juice for adults; full-fat milk for children).

Yield: 2 cups of dry mix; makes 8 beverage servings

SUNFLOWER FRUIT SMOOTHIE

This shake is adapted from one concocted by dentist Mike Lerner, of Lexington, Kentucky, who suggests it for youngsters with tooth decay problems.

½ cup All-Purpose Dynamite Mix (see above)

1 cup unsweetened fruit juice

1 ripe banana, peeled and chunked

1 medium-size apple, cut into chunks

1 tablespoon plain yogurt

Combine the dry Dynamite Mix and remaining

ingredients in a blender or food processor. Whiz until smooth.

Yield: 2 servings

Enjoy its wonderful taste now and forestall dental problems.

High-Fiber Fruity Granola

No added fat, no added sugar, no cholesterol, very rich in fiber and powerhouse nutrients—the kind we all need for sustained energy and an optimistic outlook.

½ cup raisins

½ cup dried apricots or pitted prunes, diced

1 cup fruit juice

3 cups rolled oats

½ cup sunflower seeds

½ cup soy flakes or soy nuts (optional)

¼ cup dry milk powder (optional)

½ cup wheat germ

¼ cup oat bran

½ cup lecithin granules

1 teaspoon ground cinnamon

Soak the raisins and apricots in the fruit juice for several hours or overnight. Or microwave on high for 2 minutes.

Preheat the oven to 250 degrees F.

In a large bowl, combine the remaining ingredients.

Drain the fruit juice in which the dried fruit has been soaking. Set the fruit aside, and pour the juice over the oat mixture. Mix to moisten the grains. Spread the moistened mixture thinly and evenly over 2 cookie sheets covered with parchment paper or lightly shpritzed with nonstick baking spray.

Bake for 20 minutes or until the mixture is dry and crisp. Add the reserved fruit and bake 5 minutes longer. Store in tightly-lidded containers in the refrigerator or freezer. Can be used directly from the freezer.

Microwave method: Follow the above instructions, but spread half of the moistened mixture on a sheet of parchment paper spread on the bottom of the oven or on a flat microsafe dish. Microcook, uncovered, on medium power for 5 minutes. Add the soaked fruit and cook for another minute. Stir the mixture several times during the process. Leave the granola in the oven 5 more minutes or until thoroughly dried out. Repeat the procedure with the remaining mixture.

Yield: 2 quarts

Cinnamon Oatmeal with Raisins, Nuts, and Seeds

This oatmeal, which my kids call "Oatmeal Cookie Crunch," has a wholesome sweetness and a delicious texture. The raisins, added first, sweeten the water in which the oats are cooked. The nuts and seeds provide vitamin E and sele-

2 cups water
½ cup raisins
1 cup rolled oats
½ teaspoon ground cinnamon
½ teaspoon vanilla extract
¼ cup sunflower seeds
¼ cup chopped walnuts

In a 1-quart saucepan, combine the water and raisins. Bring to a boil. Add the oats gradually, stirring as you do. Add the cinnamon and vanilla.

Reduce the heat and cook for about 8 minutes. Ladle the oatmeal into bowls and top each bowl with seeds and nuts, or offer them on the side. Children like to help themselves to the extras. Serve with milk, cream, or yogurt. For those who can't tolerate dairy products, offer soy milk or tofu, or Rice Dream, a nondairy beverage made from organic brown rice, available at health food stores.

nium, important antioxidants which have been shown to guard against cancer.

If you happen to have any oatmeal left over, refrigerate or freeze it in single-portion containers. When you or any member of your family wants a hurry-up breakfast, put it in the microwave for a minute and you've got it made.

Yield: 4 servings

Carob-Peanut-Banana Shake

If you don't have time for a sit-down breakfast, enjoy this refreshing beverage. It's a real battery-charger and can be whipped up in a jiffy.

1 cup milk

¼ cup homemade or natural peanut butter

1 mellow banana

1 tablespoon carob powder

1 tablespoon honey or molasses

In a blender or food processor, combine the ingredients and blend for about 2 minutes or until thick and frothy. If you have any of the mixture left over, pour it into small paper or plastic cups. Inset wooden sticks and freeze for a delightful afterschool snack.

Yield: 2 servings

HOT AND HEARTY OAT-BRAN CEREAL WITH BANANAS AND PECANS

This brisk breakfast will warm the cockles of your heart and delight your tastebuds. Bananas bring mellow flavor and a nice jolt of potassium, a mineral that keeps your heart in sync. Pecans provide crunch and elegance, plus iron, calcium, phosphorus, and vitamins A, B, and C. They are rich in polyunsaturated fats and high in calories. Great for skinnies, but go easy on them if you're weight-watching.

2 cups water

⅔ cup oat bran

½ teaspoon ground cinnamon

1 teaspoon grated orange rind

6 pecan halves, lightly roasted

1 mellow banana, sliced

In a saucepan, combine the water and oat bran and mix well. Add the cinnamon and orange rind. Bring to a boil, then reduce the heat and cook for about 1 minute. Ladle into two bowls, topping each bowl with sliced banana and pecan halves.

Yield: 2 servings

Sunflower Pancakes with Strawberry Applesauce

1½ cups milk

2 eggs

2 tablespoons olive or canola oil

2 tablespoons honey or molasses

1½ cups whole-wheat pastry flour

2 teaspoons baking powder

¼ cup wheat germ

¼ cup oat bran

1 tablespoon lecithin granules

3 tablespoons sunflower seeds

1 large unpeeled apple, well scrubbed and diced

1 teaspoon ground cinnamon

In a large mixing bowl or food processor, blend together the milk, eggs, oil, and sweetener.

In another bowl, mix together the flour, baking powder, wheat germ, oat bran, lecithin granules, and sunflower seeds. Combine the two mixtures gently. Do not overmix.

Sprinkle the apple with the cinnamon and fold it into the batter. For each pancake, pour ¼ cup of batter onto a hot oiled griddle over moderate heat and cook on both sides until golden brown. Serve with Strawberry Applesauce *(next recipe).*

Yield: 16 to 18 pancakes

Pancakes for breakfast make the morning special. It's nice to know that even if you're on a Spartan diet, you can indulge your passion for pancakes in good conscience. The trick is to trade in the overly sweet syrups that are associated with pancakes for delicious toppings that lower cholesterol and enhance your heart's potential.

Strawberry Applesauce

The apples in this sauce are rich in valuable fiber and pectin. Strawberries are delicious little packages of marvelous flavor, which also provide fiber and a respectable amount of vitamin C. The vitamin C is not only an antioxidant and a good friend to your arteries, it also enhances the absorption of minerals like iron, calcium, and magnesium, all important players on the heart-saver team.

1 large unpeeled apple, well scrubbed and diced

1 cup strawberries, hulled and washed

2 tablespoons fruit juice

1 tablespoon honey, or to taste

In a saucepan, combine the apple and strawberries with the juice and cook over low heat until soft. Whiz in a blender or food processor. Serve on the side or over pancakes.

Yield: 1½ cups, approximately 12 servings

Maple Walnut Oatmeal

Oatmeal can be paired with fruits, seeds, and nuts in many variations. This combination is my grandson's favorite. He says it's almost as good as an ice cream cone.

1½ cups water

⅔ cup rolled oats

2 tablespoons wheat germ

2 tablespoons chopped nuts

1 tablespoon pure maple syrup

In a saucepan, combine the water and oats. Bring to a boil, then lower the heat and simmer for 2 minutes. Stir in the wheat germ, nuts, and maple syrup. Cook for another 2 minutes or until the oatmeal reaches the desired consistency.

Microwave method: Combine all ingredients in a 4-cup glass measure and stir thoroughly. Microcook on high for 3 to 4 minutes, depending on the consistency desired. Watch carefully—oatmeal tends to boil over.

Yield: 3 servings

Goldenrod Eggs with a Happy Face

2 tablespoons unsalted butter
2 tablespoons whole-wheat pastry flour
1 cup hot milk
⅛ teaspoon black pepper
Pinch of salt (optional)
4 hard-cooked eggs
6 slices whole-grain toast
1 slice of red bell pepper
1 piece of carrot, cut into sticks
8 raisins or 4 black olives, cut in halves
Alfalfa sprouts

In a saucepan, melt the butter. Remove from the heat and stir in the flour. Cook until it bubbles. Add half of the milk all at once and the other half gradually. Bring to a boil, stirring constantly until the mixture thickens. Add the seasonings.

Separate the egg whites from the yellows. Chop

This is a very special breakfast dish, reserved for birthdays or convalescence. My Mom would make Goldenrod Eggs whenever illness jaded our appetites. Who could refuse the strengthening quality in their gold-and-white goodness? And whose spirits could not be lifted by their funny faces?

The alfalfa sprouts are a marvelous source of chlorophyll and many valuable and rare trace minerals. Alfalfa has very long roots that penetrate deep into the subsoil and pick up trace minerals that shallow-growing plants can't reach.

the egg whites and add to the white sauce.

Place 4 pieces of toast on 4 plates. (When preparing this dish for very young children, cut the toast into bite-size pieces.) Ladle the white sauce and egg white mixture over the toast. Put the egg yolks in a strainer and, with a wooden spoon, push the yolks through the strainer to make goldern hairdos on top of the egg-white mixture. Use a piece of red pepper for a smiling mouth, a piece of carrot for a Pinocchio-style nose, and raisin or black olive halves for the eyes. Alfalfa sprouts make lovely eyebrows.

Cut the remaining 2 pieces of toast in half diagonally and place a 3-cornered hat on each goldenrod head. Serve with a smile and a giggle.

Yield: 4 servings

2

Lower Your Cholesterol (With Beans and Grains)

Beans and grains—in their infinite variety—can bring new vitality to your menu. Besides being high in protein and low in calories and fat, they are an excellent source of life-enhancing minerals and soluble fiber, the kind that lowers cholesterol levels.

Dayenu? But there's more. They're easy to store and easy on the budget.

It may surprise you to learn that beans are a great food for weight-watchers. A half-cup (3.5 ounces) of cooked white or red beans provides only 118 calories. The same 3.5 ounces of choice steak provides a whopping 465 calories.

If you have shied away from cooking beans because the first step is usually "soak overnight," you can still use beans for tonight's dinner. Here's how:

> Wash a cup of dry beans and drop them into four times as much boiling water so slowly that the boiling does not stop. This causes the starch grains to burst and break the outside covering, thus enabling more rapid absorption of water and more rapid cooking. When all the beans have been added, lower the heat to a slow simmer to prevent toughening of the protein.

Here's an easy way to have presoaked beans always on hand:

> Soak a large quantity for several hours or overnight. Drain and divide them into recipe portions. Seal in plastic bags and store in the freezer. When you're ready to use the beans, there's no need to defrost.

If you are among those who get a lot of back talk from beans, there is a cooking trick that will allow you to enjoy all the wonderfully creative bean dishes without fear of embarrassing flatulence. Just discard the soak water (give it to your plants along with the first cooking water after a half-hour of cooking). In this way you are getting rid of the little guys (undigested trisaccharides) that are causing all the ruckus. Add fresh boiling water and resume cooking. Also, commercially available BEANO can be a big help.

Beans and Grains go together like Love and Marriage. They complement each other, each providing what the other needs to make a complete protein partnership.

Grains, too, are low in fat and a good source of fiber, minerals, and the B-complex vitamins. Grains should be stored in a cool dry place. Place a bay leaf in each container to retard insect infestation.

Brown Rice and Sesame Fritters

1½ cups cooked brown rice

⅓ cup sesame seeds, toasted and ground

¼ cup milk plus 2 tablespoons dry milk powder

1 egg, separated

2 tablespoons whole-wheat or soy flour

½ teaspoon herbal seasoning

Combine the rice and sesame seeds. Set aside.

In another bowl, combine the milk, milk powder, egg yolk, flour, and seasoning. Add this mixture to the rice mixture.

Beat the egg white until stiff but not dry. Fold the beaten white into the rice and sesame mixture.

Drop by the tablespoonful onto a hot griddle, lightly oiled or coated with baking spray. Brown lightly on both sides.

Yield: 3 servings, about 21 fritters

The complementary proteins of rice and sesame seeds make these fritters an ideal repast for vegetarians and those seeking heart health by cutting down on meat. Serve them with salsa, curry, or tomato-mushroom sauce, or as a finger food for a picnic or a party.

Beanburgers

2 cups cooked beans, preferably red or pink

½ cup sunflower seeds

¼ cup chopped onion

½ teaspoon chili powder

2 tablespoons olive or canola oil

3 to 4 tablespoons catsup or tomato sauce

¼ cup wheat germ

¼ cup oat bran

8 thin slices part-skim mozzarella cheese (optional)

An inexpensive and tasty morsel that we prefer to its counterpart in the beef family. The combination of beans, sunflower seeds, and wheat germ enhances the nutritional value. The cheese, if you choose to use it, provides calcium and makes the burgers irresistible to pizza-lovers.

In a food processor using the steel blade, combine the beans, sunflower seeds, onion, and chili powder. Process until smooth. Add the oil, catsup or tomato sauce, wheat germ, and oat bran and process until the ingredients are well combined.

Form into 8 small patties. Transfer to a baking sheet lightly oiled or sprayed with nonstick baking spray. Bake at 350 degrees F. for 15 to 20 minutes or until lightly browned and crusty.

If desired, put a slice of cheese on each burger and place under the broiler until the cheese melts.

Yield: 4 servings, 2 small burgers per person

BORSHT WITH BEANS

A hearty, healthful, lusty, lip-smacking dish that will elicit memories of old times. The beets and cabbage can be grated or shredded very quickly in the food processor.

8 cups vegetable broth or water

1 medium-size onion, chopped

2 cups coarsely grated raw beets

2 cups coarsely shredded cabbage

1 to 1½ cups cooked pinto beans

1 tablespoon lemon juice

Freshly ground pepper and herbal seasoning to taste

Reduced-fat sour cream or plain yogurt for topping

In a large saucepan, bring the broth or water to a boil. Add the onion and beets. Cook for 15 to 20 minutes or until just tender. Add the cabbage and drained beans. Cook for 10 minutes. Add the lemon juice and seasonings. Serve with a dollop of sour cream or yogurt on each bowl of borsht.

Yield: 6 to 8 bowlfuls

Mushroom, Barley, and Bean Soup

½ cup large dry lima beans

¼ cup mung beans

¼ cup coarse barley

2 quarts water or stock

1 pound soup meat

3 marrow bones

1 large onion, sliced

1 cup finely chopped carrot

1 turnip or ½ rutabaga, peeled and chopped

1 tablespoon chopped fresh dill weed or ½ teaspoon dried

½ cup chopped fresh parsley or 2 tablespoons dried

½ teaspoon celery salt (optional)

2 tablespoons nutritional yeast

2 teaspoons reduced-sodium Tamari soy sauce

1 teaspoon powdered kelp

Herbal seasoning and ground pepper to taste

Prepare this on Friday and you'll have an excellent meal-in-a-dish for Shabbat. The barley gives this soup a hearty, creamy, chewy texture that makes you think it's fattening. Not so. Barley has less fat and more iron than brown rice. You can enjoy a half-cup of cooked barley—with all its calcium, potassium, and niacin—at a cost of only 52 calories.

The nutritional (brewer's) yeast contributes fabulous nutrients. It is rich in *all the B vitamins, even B_{12}, which is very hard to come by in nonanimal foods. Nutritional yeast is 50 percent protein and is the richest dietary source of chromium, which helps the body regulate blood sugar and may help to prevent diabetes as well as treat it.*

Wash the beans and barley and place in a soup kettle with the water or stock and remaining ingredients. Cover and bring to a boil. Allow to simmer gently for about 2 hours, until the beans are soft. Remove the meat. Cut it into serving portions. Serve the soup with a piece of the meat in each bowl.

Note: This soup can be a hearty vegetarian soup. Just omit the meat and bones.

Yield: 8 to 10 servings

SPICY BEAN MUFFINS

Sound strange? You won't believe how delicious bean muffins can be. With their high fiber, oat bran, and lecithin granules (which have been shown to emulsify clots), these muffins are practically a prescription for heart health.

1 cup cooked and mashed pinto beans (½ cup dry beans will yield 1 cup cooked. The beans can be "mashed" with a little of the cooking water in your blender or food processor.)

1 egg or 2 egg whites

2 tablesoons olive or canola oil

1 teaspoon vanilla extract

2 tablespoons molasses or honey

½ cup minus 2 tablespoons sifted whole-wheat pastry flour

4 tablespoons oat bran

2 tablespoons lecithin granules

½ teaspoon baking soda

½ teaspoon ground cinnamon

⅛ teaspoon grated nutmeg

1 cup diced apples

½ cup raisins

¼ cup chopped nuts

In a mixing bowl or food processor, combine the beans, egg or egg whites, oil, vanilla, and molasses or honey.

In another bowl, combine the flour, oat bran, lecithin, baking soda, and spices.

Preheat the oven to 350 degrees F. Grease or spray with nonstick cooking spray 12 regular-size muffin wells, or line with paper or foil cups.

Add the dry ingredients to the bean mixture and mix briefly to combine. Stir in the apples, raisins, and nuts. Spoon the batter into the muffin wells and bake for 20 minutes.

Yield: 12 magnificent muffins

Brown Rice, Cheese, and Nut Loaf

When it comes to rice, brown is beautiful. Enjoy its high fiber, low fat, low sodium, and energizing B vitamins in this delightful medley of tastes and textures. You can slice this loaf when it cools, then top with a little tomato sauce and grated cheese and broil. So who needs pizza?

1 onion, chopped
3 stalks celery with tops, chopped
½ cup chopped cashews
½ cup chopped walnuts
½ cup sunflower seeds
1 cup cooked brown rice
1 cup lowfat cottage or ricotta cheese
2 teaspoons chopped chives or green onions (scallions)
2 tablespoons chopped parsley
1 tablespoon crushed dried thyme or 2 tablespoons fresh
2 eggs, lightly beaten
½ cup wheat germ
¼ cup sesame seeds

In a microwave-safe bowl, combine the onion and celery. Cover and microcook on high for 2 minutes or until soft. Alternatively, sauté the onion and celery in a bit of oil over medium heat until the onion is translucent.

In a mixing bowl, combine the nuts, seeds, rice, cheese, chives or green onions, parsley, thyme, and beaten eggs. Mix to combine. Add the onion and celery mixture.

Grease or spray with nonstick baking spray a 9-inch loaf pan. Sprinkle half the wheat germ on the bottom and sides. Turn the mixture into the pan and sprinkle the remaining wheat germ and the sesame seeds on top. Bake for 1 hour at 350 degrees F.

Yield: 6 to 8 servings

KOSHER PAREVE SAUSAGE

Three different kinds of beans and lots of spices make these the kind of snack food kids love. All of us can enjoy these crunchy "sausages" for their cancer-inhibiting value. Soybeans, it has been shown by Harvard University researcher Ann Kennedy, D. Sc.,

2 cups cooked soybeans

1 cup cooked dry lima beans

1 cup cooked dry navy beans

1 tablespoon olive or canola oil

2 teaspoons herbal seasoning

¼ teaspoon each of crushed dried marjoram, thyme, sage, and summer savory

½ teaspoon paprika

1 large egg or 2 small

⅔ cup milk

1 cup cornmeal

Preheat the oven to 500 degrees F. Mash all the beans in a foodmill or processor. Add the oil and all of the seasonings. Shape the mixture into sausage-like rolls.

Combine the egg and milk in a bowl. Dip the sausages into this mixture, then into the cornmeal. Place them in a large shallow roasting pan that has been greased with oil or nonstick spray. Bake for 10 minutes, turning occasionally until the sausages are browned on all sides.

Yield: 6 servings

may help cells in a precancerous stage revert to normal.

Peaches and Pasta

1 teaspoon unsalted butter

2 tablespoons tomato paste

2 tablespoons dry red wine

1 package (8 ounces) **macaroni or shells,** cooked

2 fresh peaches, peeled and halved

1 cup blueberries, picked over and rinsed

¼ cup grated mozzarella cheese

In a small saucepan, melt the butter. Stir in the tomato paste and wine. Add to the cooked pasta and stir to mix well.

Spoon this mixture into 4 ovenproof dishes. Top each with a peach half and some blueberries. Sprinkle with cheese. Bake in a 350-degree F. oven for 10 minutes or until the cheese melts and the sauce bubbles.

Yield: 4 servings

A lovely summer meal—a sure pickup for lagging appetites. Serve it on the patio and savor it slowly to prolong the pleasure of the medley of exotic flavors and textures.

A peach is indeed a nutritional bargain when it comes to calories—only 38 calories for all that goodness.

Kasha, Vegetable, and Cheese Skillet

Kasha (buckwheat) is used like a grain but is actually a member of the rhubarb family. It is very rich in potassium (352 mg in a cup) and very low in sodium (only 1 mg in a cup), making it a great food for your heart and your blood pressure. Its robust bone-warming quality makes it ideal for cold wintry days. Its hearty flavor hits the spot any day.

4 tablespoons tomato juice

1 large onion, chopped

1 stalk celery, sliced

2 green or red bell peppers, chopped

1 cup sliced mushrooms

1 cup uncooked coarse kasha

2 cups vegetable stock or water

1 cup cottage cheese, drained

1 cup corn (fresh, frozen, or canned)

4 to 6 thin slices of part-skim mozzarella cheese

10 cherry tomatoes and parsley sprigs for garnish

In a large ovenproof skillet with a tight-fitting lid, heat the tomato juice and cook the onion, celery, peppers, and mushrooms for about 3 minutes. Add the kasha and the stock or water and bring to a boil, then reduce the heat to low.

Cover and cook for 10 minutes. Turn off the heat and mix in the cottage cheese and corn. Place the mozzarella cheese on top and slide the skillet under the broiler, or microwave just until the cheese melts. Garnish with cherry tomatoes and sprigs of parsley.

Yield: 8 to 10 servings

3

Grow Your Own Sprouts (Multiply Your Antioxidants)

ou can stay young and vital all the days of your life, a doctor once told me, if every day you eat something which, if put into the ground, would grow.

Knishes, kugels, and blintzes are all a pleasure to eat and should be enjoyed. But, if you put them into the ground, would they grow? Hardly.

What then can you eat which, if put into the ground, *would* grow?

The answer is—seeds. A seed is the very essence of life. All life starts from seed. It has been noted that Nature is careless of the individual but careful of the species. Therefore, the seed, which is Nature's instrument of perpetuity, gets the best of everything. The seed will pull from the soil all the elements necessary to produce a new plant. It contains more vital nutrients than the plant from which it comes.

But what kind of seeds can you eat? Sunflower, pumpkin, caraway, squash, watermelon, sesame seeds—all are edible. They can also be used in many delectable dishes. There are many other seeds that are probably finding their way into your trash can when they could be adding vitality to your meals and to you.

The next time you cut a pepper, regard those seeds with new respect. They contain the vital factor capable of producing a new plant. Add them to your salad, your stew, your soup. Do not discard cucumber, tomato, or eggplant seeds.

Seeds are great—but sprouts are better! A sprout is a seed in the act of creation. In a seed, the life force is dormant. But, give that seed the proper conditions—air and water—and it will wake up, stretch, and burst into life. It becomes a sprout, gloriously alive. And while exulting in self-creation, it produces almost every element essential to sustain and nurture life.

When the seed explodes to release its vital force, it multiplies its vitamin values and develops some vitamins that were not in the original seed. Grains, for instance, contain no vitamin C. Sprouted grains, however, do. In fact, sprouted soybeans were used during World War II to prevent scurvy because citrus fruit and other sources of vitamin C were very scarce.

Whole grains and beans are good foods and have their place in your dietary plan. But, these foods reach their peak when they are sprouted.

Sprouts are your wisest investment, nutritionally and economically. One pound of mung beans cost less than two dollars and will yield eight pounds of sprouts. Eight pounds of these lightweight dynamos would practically fill your bathtub.

As they grow, their vitamin, antioxidant, and protein content increase. Most sprouts have 12 percent more protein than their parent seeds. Their B vitamins jump three to ten times. Like magic, sprouting actually creates vitamin C, an important antioxidant, even when the parent seeds have none.

The growing sprout uses up the starch in the seed, making them very low in calories. A whole cup of alfalfa sprouts has only 10 calories; a cup of mung beans has only 32.

And get this: Wheat sprouts, because they are empowered with several antioxidants, have been shown to inhibit the genetic damage in cells caused by free radicals.

So, what are you waiting for? You can raise a crop of sprouts in three days and you don't need a spade, rake, or sun hat. You can grow them anywhere, even in the trunk of your car.

Here's how you do it.

Get some organically-raised grains, seeds, legumes—wheat, rye, alfalfa, mung beans, garbanzo, soybeans, radish, parsley, cress, and so forth. Don't get them from a garden supply store. Seeds meant for planting in the ground are usually treated with fungicides. Get your seeds, grains, and beans from food stores, preferably natural food stores that cater to the needs of the sprouter.

I like to keep three jars of sprouts growing at the same time: a bean, a grain, and a small seed. Their protein patterns complement each other.

So let's start:

Put two tablespoons of alfalfa seeds in a strainer, give them a quick rinse to remove surface dust, then place them in a quart jar. Half fill the jar with tepid water. Cover and let it stand overnight. Follow the same procedure using three tablespoons of wheat berries in one jar and three tablespoons of lentils or mung beans in another. Mung beans become what is commonly known as the "chop suey" sprout. Let the jars stand overnight.

Next morning, cover each jar with a double layer of cheesecloth or nylon net secured with a rubber band, or make screened lids from window screening cut to fit canning jar rings. Lids with mesh screening are available at natural food stores.

Now, without removing the covers, simply drain off the soak water into a jar. *Do not discard it.* It is a rich source of nutrients. Use it to start potatoes, or rice—or to steam vegetables in your wok instead of frying with oil. If you have more soak water than you can use in a few days, freeze it in ice cube trays, then dump the cubes into a plastic bag. Label them "Dynamite" and enjoy visions of rosy good health every time you use them.

Next, rinse the seeds and grains with tepid water. Feed the rinse water to your plants. They like it better than sweet talk. After rinsing, let the jars rest, slightly tilted so that any moisture can escape but a source of oxygen remains. Bear in mind that sprouting seeds, grains, and beans like to be moist but not wet. They should never sit in puddles.

Now, put them in a dark place. I put mine under the sink, where the hot water pipe warms the atmosphere. If this is not practical, rest them on the sink, slightly tilted (place a sponge or a folded dishcloth under the bottom edge of the jar), and cover the whole shebang with a towel. The idea is to keep out the light. All things germinate best in the dark. Modesty, I guess.

Repeat the rinsing procedure two or three times each day. By the end of the second day, your wheat and lentils will be just about ready. In cold weather, they may require more time. Don't let wheat sprouts grow any longer than the grain. Not that they are bad when they get longer; they just don't taste as good as the shorter sprouts. If the sprouts do get longer than you like, spread them on a cookie sheet and place it in the oven heated only to warm. When the sprouts are dry, grind them in a blender or food processor and use as flour.

Alfalfa takes a little longer. As soon as two tiny leaves appear, on about the third day, bring your alfalfa into the light. They will be a lovely green, overflowing with chlorophyll (a blood purifier) and ready to be enjoyed.

Be sure to eat the whole thing: root, seed, and sprout.

Sprouting the Larger Beans

The larger beans—like garbanzo and soy—need lots of room. Don't crowd them.

First step: Soak about half a cup of beans in a bowl or jar. Use plenty of water because they will triple in volume. Next morning, pour off the liquid. Remove any broken beans; they won't sprout.

Rinse the beans and spread them out in a colander. Now, dampen a dishtowel and place it on top of the beans. Slip the whole thing into a plastic bag in order to retain some moisture, but leave it open to insure a source of oxygen. Remove the plastic bag and dishtowel and rinse three times a day with tepid water. Garbanzos are ready in two to three days. Soybeans take a little longer. Be sure to pick out those beans that are broken, shriveled, or discolored—and any which fail to sprout. If you have many of this kind, you may need a fresh supply. Old beans are not good sprouters.

Store your sprouts in the refrigerator and use within a few days. If you can't use them up while they're fresh, then dry them. Grind them and use as a base for a superior breading mix.

During the winter, when lettuce is limp and high-priced, use alfalfa sprouts on the sandwiches you send to school or office. They remain fresh and vibrant for several hours and bring the lovely taste of "springtime in the garden" to your lunch hour.

How Do You Use Sprouts?

Let me count the ways: on breakfast cereal and scrambled eggs; in fresh salads and stir-fry dishes; sprinkled on soups; in meatloaf and hamburgers; in breads, biscuits, cupcakes, or muffins; in kugels, blintzes, and knishes; blended into healthful beverages or as a snack. Since they have very few calories, they make a great TV nosh for waist-watchers.

Sprouts are unequaled as a garnish or topping. When you float them in a bowl of soup, they add a touch of freshness. Sprinkle lentil sprouts over steamed vegetables, mung beans sprouts on potato salad, wheat sprouts on pea soup, rye sprouts on potato soup. Add rye sprouts to brown rice and you have "mock wild rice," which makes a wonderful stuffing for fowl.

Lentils have a pleasant peppery taste and can be used instead of celery and green pepper in your stews, soups, and casseroles.

Alfalfa and wheat sprouts, when dried, are sweet and crunchy and can be used to replace nuts in your baked goods.

Combine sprouts with fruits for superior gelatin salads.

Blend the sprouts of your choice with an equal amount of hot water. Season with herbs and garnish with watercress or parsley for a delicious body-warming soup. Lentil sprouts are particularly tasty this way.

Increase your culinary expertise with recipes featuring seeds and sprouts.

PAPAYA SEED PEPPER

The seeds of papaya have a pungent peppery flavor and are super-rich in enzymes and other valuable nutrients.

To make papaya pepper, remove the seeds from the papaya. Place them with the filaments attached in a very low oven, in the microwave on low, or on a warm radiator until they are dry. Discard the fibrous material and put the seeds in your pepper mill. Add a few grinds to those foods you like to pepper.

PUMPKIN SEEDS

Pumpkin seeds are not only delicious, they are a good source of zinc—an essential mineral associated with the sense of taste and smell, the ability to heal, the control of acne, fertility, and the health of the prostate gland.

To make your own edible pumpkin seeds, remove the seeds and fibrous material from the cavity of the pumpkin. Slowly dry them in the oven or microwave. Discard the fibrous material, reserving the seeds for happy munching.

Apple-Sesame-Nut Salad

A Waldorf salad with an extra dimension.

4 tablespoons sesame seeds

4 medium-size unpeeled apples, scrubbed and diced

4 stalks celery, diced

½ cup chopped walnuts

1 cup plain yogurt

Toast the sesame seeds in a cast-iron skillet over medium heat or in the microwave for 1 minute on high. In a bowl, combine the other ingredients. Mix with the toasted seeds and serve on a bed of greens.

Yield: 4 to 6 servings

Peaches-and-Cheese Alfalfa Sandwiches

Peaches are not only beautiful to behold and heavenly to eat, they provide fiber and the antioxidants beta carotene and vitamin C to help prevent cancer and heart disease. Besides, their sodium-to-potassium ratio is just what the doctor ordered to prevent high blood pressure.

4 or 5 fresh peaches, pitted

½ cup cream cheese, preferably Neufchâtel or yogurt cream cheese

1 cup cottage cheese

½ cup chopped walnuts, lightly roasted

½ teaspoon grated lemon or orange rind

1 unpeeled apple, scrubbed and diced

8 slices whole-grain bread

3 cups alfalfa sprouts

Cut one peach into 8 slices. Chop the remaining peaches into small pieces. In a large bowl, combine the cream cheese, cottage cheese, walnuts,

Alfalfa is one of the rare plant sources for vitamin B_{12} (cobalamin). B_{12} is necessary for the formation of red blood cells.

❧

and lemon or orange rind. Fold in the chopped peaches and diced apple. Spread this mixture on the bread slices. Sprinkle each open-faced sandwich generously with alfalfa sprouts, then top each with a peach slice.

To delight the small fry, cut up another peach into 8 slices and make a mouth and eyebrows with the slices. Use a walnut or piece of carrot for the nose. Use the alfalfa sprouts to make a healthy crop of hair and whiskers. This is a great dish for children's parties.

Yield: 8 servings

Wheat or Triticale Sprout Confections

Triticale is a grain, the "child" of a wheat "mother" and a rye "father." It surpasses both "parents" in protein content and has a hearty nutty flavor. Both wheat and triticale sprouts are an excellent source of vitamin E, a powerful antioxidant shown to inhibit tumor formation.

❧

1 cup wheat or triticale sprouts

1 cup coarsely chopped pecans or walnuts or sunflower seeds

1 cup raisins

1 tablespoon honey

Unsweetened coconut flakes or sesame seeds

Chop the sprouts, nuts or seeds, and raisins. Use a food chopper, food processor, or wooden chopping bowl. Add the honey and mix well. Form into 1-inch balls and roll them in the coconut or sesame seeds. Get the children in on the rolling. A few will roll right into their eager mouths, and that's just fine.

Yield: 32 Sprout Confections

Festive Figs

12 dried figs
¼ cup chopped almonds
½ cup wheat sprouts
¼ cup wheat germ
½ cup dry sherry
Unsweetened coconut flakes or sesame seeds

Make a slit in each fig. Combine the almonds, sprouts, and wheat germ. Stuff each fig with this mixture. Place the stuffed figs in a bowl and cover with the dry sherry. (As a substitute for sherry, try cranberry, apple, or pineapple juice, or apricot nectar.) Let stand for 24 hours or more. Turn occasionally so all figs get well soaked. Drain. Roll them lightly in the coconut flakes or sesame seeds.

Yield: 12 Festive Figs

The exceptional health value of the fig has been known since antiquity. It is one of the few fruits that is more alkaline than acid, due to its large content of minerals: iron for protection against anemia; blood-building copper, which has antioxidant value; tissue-strengthening manganese and iodine, so important to the thyroid gland.

Rainbow Salad

2 cups spinach leaves, rinsed well and cut up, **or 2 cups mung bean sprouts**
2 medium-size unpeeled carrots, well scrubbed and grated
2 unpeeled turnips, well scrubbed and grated
1 unpeeled beet, well scrubbed and grated
Your favorite low-fat salad dressing *(see index for recipes)*

This salad should be prescribed by doctors, it is so rich in antioxidants. Each colorful vegetable contributes its special nutrients to this pyramid of natural goodness. Raw spinach and carrots provide lots of beta carotene to help reduce the risk of cancer. Turnips, a member of the crucifer family, are a good source of fiber and vitamin C. Beets, sweet red jewels, provide lots of potassium to lower blood pressure.

Arrange the spinach leaves or sprouts in the bottom of a large glass salad bowl. Cover with a thin layer of grated carrot. Spread a thin layer of the grated turnip on top, followed by the grated beet. Top the pyramid with a spoonful of the salad dressing or serve the dressing on the side.

Yield: 4 servings

The black radish, highly prized in Egypt in the days of the Pharaohs, is a member of the cruciferous cabbage family, which provides unique nutrients called indoles, especially valued for their ability to detoxify carcinogens.

BLACK RADISH SALAD

1 black radish, peeled

1 medium-size onion

1 teaspoon chicken fat

Salt and pepper to taste (optional)

½ cup alfalfa sprouts

Grate the radish and onion in the food processor or by hand into a small bowl. Add the fat and the seasoning if desired. Mix well. Top with alfalfa sprouts.

Yield: 2 to 4 servings

RAW BEET RELISH

2 cups shredded peeled raw beets

½ cup sprouted garbanzos

½ cup lemon juice or cider vinegar

½ teaspoon each of crushed dried oregano, thyme, and basil

1 tablespoon reduced-sodium Tamari soy sauce

2 tablespoons grated horseradish

Combine all ingredients. Keep refrigerated in a covered jar.

Yield: 2½ cups

A wonderful relish for meat or fish. Though it's easier to peel cooked beets, you can peel and eat them raw and enjoy twice as much vitamin C for extra antioxidant protection.

The horseradish in this relish is also an excellent source of vitamin C. Its pungent aroma helps clear the sinuses.

APRICOT-ALMOND RAW JAM

½ cup dried apricots

8 whole almonds

½ cup wheat sprouts

½ cup raisins

Apple juice to cover

Grated orange peel (optional)

Place the apricots, almonds, sprouts, and raisins in a jar. Cover with apple juice. Let stand for 24 hours in the refrigerator, or place in the microwave on medium for 2 minutes. Place the soaked fruit-and-nut combination in a blender or food processor, adding the grated orange peel if desired, and whiz until smooth.

Yield: 1 cup

Hippocrates must have had both apricots and almonds in mind when he said, "Let food be your medicine." Apricots are packed with beta carotene and fiber. Beta carotene, the plant form of vitamin A, has been shown to have anticancer activity.

4

How to Be a Healthy Vegetarian

Statistically, vegetarians in the United States are more slender, healthier, and longer-lived than meat-eaters. Why?

Because their greater use of grains, vegetables, fruits, seeds, and nuts increases their intake of essential nutrients while reducing their consumption of calories and saturated fats. Judaism recognizes the superior benefits of a nonmeat diet. In fact, the killing of animals is justified only with great hesitation—and some misgivings. The *shochet* (ritual slaughterer) sheds a tear.

The Talmud, referring to Deuteronomy 14:26, says, "Man should not eat meat unless he has a special craving for it, and even then, only occasionally and sparingly." Also in the Talmud: "The longevity of the generations from Adam to Noah is due to their vegetarian diet."

Zerubbabel attributes the good morals and keen intellect of the Hebrews to their scant eating of meat.

But, there are Jewish traditions that make it hard for one to be both an observant Jew and a vegetarian. Also in the Talmud is a description of the ways a Jew celebrates Passover, Shavuot, and Sukkot: "There is no happiness without meat."

One could define the word "meat" in its figurative sense, as meaning food in general, but the association of meat with celebrations is so strong that some *halachic* (those who strictly adhere to Jewish law) vegetarians do eat a symbolic piece of chicken on festive occasions.

The word *vegetarian* is not, as one might think, derived from vegetable, but from the Latin *vegetus,* which means "whole, sound, fresh, lively." Whether you are a *halachic* vegetarian, an ethical vegetarian, the mother of a vegetarian, or a meat-eater seeking to reduce meat consumption, or if you would simply enjoy a change of direction in your diet, let me assure you that it is possible to maintain a sound, healthy, vigorous physical state on a purely vegetarian regimen. It's also possible to enjoy some great meals—but you should have at least a rudimentary knowledge of protein patterns.

One of the dangers inherent in the vegetarian diet is the possibility of an imbalance in amino acids, the building blocks of protein. Eggs, dairy products, meat, and fish are complete proteins, which means they contain all the essential amino acids in the correct proportions. Because amino acids depend on each other to make body tissue, if one is absent none of them is used. It's like trying to make brick without straw.

When people in the Deep South lived mainly on a diet of corn, the dreaded disease pellagra became endemic. Corn is low in the amino acid tryptophan, which the body needs to manufacture niacin, an essential B vitamin.

So what's the formula? Here's a simple guide suggested by Dr. Roger J. Williams, author of *Nutrition Against Disease* (Pitman, New York):

> Don't restrict yourself to one part of an organism, try to get the whole works. In the plant world, do not restrict yourself to green leaves (spinach, kale, romaine, endive) or to roots (parsnips, turnips, carrots, potatoes) or to seeds (corn, wheat, rye) or to fruit (apples, tomatoes). Each of these is in itself incomplete. A combination diet consisting of leaves, roots, tubers, seeds, and fruits is a vast improvement.

Helpful hint: Nuts, seeds, avocados, whole grains, and legumes are considered incomplete proteins. But, according to Dr. Williams's formula, when eaten with raw green leafy vegetables, they provide a complete protein well used by the body.

Raw foods such as salads, fresh fruits, and sprouts are important in everyone's diet, vegetarian or not, but they have particular importance for the vegetarian because some essential amino acids, particularly lysine, are heat sensitive.

To insure yourself a complete amino acid pattern, make sure that with every meal of cooked food you have either raw salad greens, raw sprouts, raw fruit, or unroasted seeds.

More helpful hints:

- Beans and grains have complementary protein patterns. Whenever you use wheat flour (made from a grain), one-fifth should be soy flour (made from a bean). Take note of the ratio: five parts grain to one part legume.
- When you cook brown rice (a grain), add some lentils, split peas, or mung beans to the pot. About three tablespoons of beans to one cup of rice.
- Cook lentils with barley or rice.
- Cook split peas with cracked wheat or bulgur.
- Add cracked wheat to chili beans.
- Serve chili beans with polenta (cornmeal).
- If you use dry skim milk, make sure you get the kind that is spray-dried. When skim milk is subjected to intense heat, as it is in dry milk that is not spray-dried, important amino acids—lysine, methionine, and valine—are destroyed.
- When you serve nuts for noshing, mix them up. Cashews are high in lysine, Brazil nuts are a good source of methionine, as are sunflower and sesame seeds. Combine nuts with raisins for a more complete protein pattern. Remember the song *Rozhinkes mit Mandlin* ("Raisins and Almonds")? The old folks sure knew their aminos.

Get Some B_{12}

The one essential vitamin sometimes in short supply in a vegetarian diet is B_{12}, which is associated with animal proteins. *Lacto-ovo* vegetarians, who eat eggs and dairy products, are not quite so vulnerable as are *vegans,* who avoid all animal byproducts.

Pernicious anemia in vegetarians frequently escapes diagnosis. That is because the vegetarian diet is rich in green vegetables, which provide lots of the B vitamin folic acid. The folic acid, an essential nutrient, which has been shown to prevent neurological defects in babies whose mothers consumed it before becoming pregnant, keeps the blood picture looking normal and thus masks the presence of pernicious anemia so that irreparable nerve damage can occur before the B_{12} deficiency is discovered.

Nutritional yeast, wheat germ, soybeans, sunflower seeds, and sprouted garbanzos do have some B_{12}. But to be nutritionally safe, it would be wise for everyone on a vegetarian diet to take a daily vitamin B supplement that provides B_{12}, thereby avoiding the possibility of neurologic damage which might not reveal symptoms for five years. B_{12} is not synthetic or of animal origin. It is made from molds.

Can you enjoy a vegetarian diet and still get back to your ancestral roots? You sure can. Back in the *shtetl,* where meat was a rare commodity, many delicious meatless dishes were devised. Traditional kugels, blintzes, kreplach, and kasha varnishkes are all examples of dishes containing complementary amino acids that form complete proteins. But, consider that in those days flour was not refined. Our ancestors used whole-grain flour, which provided important values that are lacking in today's refined flour and in the foods made from it.

If you use whole-wheat flour or add wheat germ and a little soy to a lukshen kugel made with cheese and eggs, it will provide more and better protein than you get in a pastrami sandwich.

Enjoy the taste and health values of the delicious vegetarian dishes in this chapter. They are all nutritionally balanced to give you complete proteins. Many other vegetarian recipes appear throughout the book. See the index for recipes.

VEGETABLE SOUP WITH WALNUT DUMPLINGS

Walnut dumplings, seasoned with garlic, parsley, sage, and marjoram and fortified with the yolk of an egg, give this hearty vegetable soup an extra culinary dimension.

FOR THE SOUP:

2 quarts water or vegetable stock

1 carrot, scrubbed and cut into chunks

1 parsnip or parsley root, scrubbed and cut into chunks

3 small unpeeled potatoes, scrubbed and cut into quarters

2 ribs celery with tops, cut into 1-inch pieces

1 clove garlic, minced

2 onions, cut into quarters

1 teaspoon no-salt herbal seasoning

Freshly ground pepper to taste

FOR THE DUMPLINGS:

1 tablespoon canola oil, olive oil, or butter

2 tablespoons finely minced onion

¼ cup whole-wheat, rye, or spelt flour

¼ cup wheat germ

1 egg yolk

½ cup cold water

Pinch of garlic powder

Pinch of freshly ground pepper

1 slice whole-grain bread, soaked in water then pressed out and torn into small pieces

2 tablespoons finely chopped walnuts

1 tablespoon finely chopped parsley

Pinch of dried marjoram or sage

1 egg white, beaten to soft peaks

3 cups water

TO MAKE THE SOUP:

In a large soup pot, heat the water or stock. Add the next 8 ingredients. Cover, bring to a boil, and simmer for 1 hour.

TO MAKE THE DUMPLINGS:

In a medium-size skillet, heat the oil or butter. Add the minced onion and sauté till golden. Sprinkle the flour and wheat germ over the onions and cook briefly.

In a bowl, beat the egg yolk with the cold water; add the garlic powder and pepper. Add this mixture to the onion mixture. Add the soaked bread, chopped nuts, parsley, and marjoram or sage. Let stand for 15 minutes, then fold in the beaten egg white.

In a saucepan, bring the 3 cups of water to a boil. With a spoon, take ½ tablespoon of the dumpling mixture and ease it into the boiling water. Repeat until the mixture is used up. Reduce the heat and simmer for 15 minutes, until the dumplings are light and fluffy. Remove the dumplings with a slotted spoon. Place a few in each soup bowl, and spoon the vegetables and soup over them.

Yield: 6 to 8 servings

LENTIL-MILLET LOAF

The combination of lentils (a bean) and millet (a grain) makes this a nicely balanced and delicious preparation—a favorite among vegetarians. Apple, carrot, and soy enhance the flavor and nutrient value of this one-dish meal.

1½ cups cooked lentils (½ cup brown lentils and ½ teaspoon herbal seasoning added to 1½ cups water and cooked for 30 minutes)

1 cup cooked millet (¼ cup millet and ¼ teaspoon herbal seasoning added slowly to 1 cup boiling water and cooked over low heat for 30 minutes)

2 eggs

1 unpeeled apple, well scrubbed and cut up

½ cup grated carrot

1 tablespoon sesame or canola oil

½ cup soybean granules

1 teaspoon kelp

½ teaspoon herbal seasoning

½ teaspoon dried parsley or chives

2 tablespoons toasted sesame seeds

Combine all ingredients except the sesame seeds in mixing bowl or food processor and process briefly. Pour the mixture into a 9 x 5–inch loaf pan, lightly oiled or shpritzed with a nonstick spray. Sprinkle with the sesame seeds. Bake for 45 minutes, uncovered, in a preheated 375-degree F. oven or microwave on high for about 10 minutes.

Yield: 6 to 8 servings

Kasha and Sesame Seed Patties

1 teaspoon canola oil or chicken fat

1 medium-size onion, thinly sliced

1 cup chopped mushrooms

1 cup coarse-grain kasha (buckwheat groats), cooked

1 tablespoon chopped fresh parsley

2 tablespoons sesame seeds

2 eggs

In a skillet, heat the oil or chicken fat and lightly sauté the onion and mushrooms for about 3 minutes. Add this mixture to the cooked kasha. In a mixing bowl or with a food processor, beat together the parsley, sesame seeds, and eggs. Combine with the kasha.

Form into 3-inch patties and sauté on both sides in a hot oiled skillet, or bake in a 350-degree F. oven for about 10 minutes or until crisp on the outside but still moist on the inside. Serve in warm rolls with mustard, hot tomato sauce, or pickled relish. Great for a vegetarian picnic.

Yield: 8 patties

A vegetarian burger that rivals the original for popularity.

Mushrooms add much more than a touch of class and incomparable flavor to these patties. Mushrooms are rich in pantothenate, the antistress vitamin. They are also rich in niacin and riboflavin, are a good source of copper and selenium, the antioxidant mineral that helps you stay young longer, and provide trace amounts of magnesium and zinc. And there are only 20 calories in a cup of mushrooms.

SUNFLOWER PATTIES

The sunflower seed is like a little sunlamp in your digestive system. It is one of the few foods that provide the sunshine vitamin D, so necessary to the utilization of calcium and phosphorus, both of which are plentiful in the sunflower seed. Its high protein content (24 percent) makes it an excellent substitute for meat.

1 tablespoon canola or olive oil

3 tablespoons chopped onion

1 clove garlic, minced

½ cup finely chopped mushrooms

½ cup chopped celery, including leaves

½ cup grated raw carrot

2 tablespoons chopped green pepper

⅓ cup water or vegetable broth

1 egg

1 cup ground sunflower seeds

2 tablespoons wheat germ

2 tablespoons chopped fresh parsley or 1 teaspoon dried

½ teaspoon powdered kelp

¼ teaspoon dry mustard

1 teaspoon chopped fresh basil or ½ teaspoon dried

2 teaspoons reduced-sodium Tamari soy sauce

¼ cup tomato sauce, or as much as needed to bind the ingredients

In a large skillet, heat the oil and sauté the onion, garlic, mushrooms, celery, carrot, and pepper for 2 minutes. Add the water or broth, cover the skillet, and allow to steam-sauté over medium heat for 3 minutes. Turn the skillet ingredients into a large bowl and add the remaining ingredients.

Preheat the oven to 350 degrees F.

Mix the ingredients well. Form into patties about the size of hamburgers and arrange them in an oiled shallow baking dish about 10 x 6 inches.

Bake until brown, about 20 minutes. Turn and brown the other side, about 10 minutes.

VARIATIONS:

- Coat with sesame seeds before baking.
- Patties may be sautéed or broiled.
- Try broiling with Cheddar cheese on top.

Yield: 8 patties

5

EXPAND YOUR VEGETABLE HORIZONS

For many years we have endured untold suffering and invested oodles of money in search of a cancer cure. We still don't have a cure, but now at least we know more about the nutritional path to PREVENTION. The magic bullet is the antioxidants, the substances that are your first line of defense against free radical damage.

Free radicals are singlet oxygen molecules, substances with unpaired electrons desperately seeking a mate. Like the unfaithful, they latch onto someone else's mate, which renders the other guy a singlet—who in turn latches onto another, causing a chain reaction that is devastating to the cells of the body.

It is now thought that almost every devastating condition known to humankind can be triggered by free radicals. And since free radicals are the enemy, antioxidants are nutritional heroes.

Just consider: More than 300 studies have shown that vitamin A and its precursor, beta carotene, and other carotenoids seem to inhibit the development of cancer. The best food sources of vitamin A are liver, eggs, fish oils, and dairy products, especially butter. Healthy amounts of beta carotene and other carotenoids are found in yams, carrots, tomatoes, papayas, peaches, cantaloupe, spinach, and broccoli. Not only do these nutrients protect against cancer, they help you to feel and look younger longer.

Vitamin A is the most important vitamin for a soft, smooth, healthy, blemish-free complexion and good eyesight. Because vitamin A is insoluble in water and remains stable at ordinary cooking temperatures, very little of the vitamin is lost in cooking. However, exposure to air and sunlight can cause a serious loss of the vitamin. Fruits, vegetables, butter, and other vitamin A-rich foods should therefore be stored at low temperatures away from direct light, as in a refrigerator. If fats are rancid or vegetables wilted, most of the vitamin A has been destroyed.

If you have vegetable scorners at your house, try the three pudding recipes that follow and you'll be blessing them with health insurance in tasty dishes they can't resist.

To make these dairy recipes pareve, substitute oil for the butter and fruit juice for the milk. To make them fleishig, substitute oil or chicken fat for the butter and chicken broth for the milk.

BROCCOLI PUDDING

This Broccoli Pudding is so tasty, even George Bush would enjoy it. A layer of vegetables rises to the top during baking, while a tasty pudding layer forms in the middle.

1½ cups cooked broccoli, drained

1 tablespoon butter, melted

¼ teaspoon crushed dried oregano

⅛ teaspoon pepper

1 teaspoon salt-free herbal seasoning

⅓ cup oat bran or wheat germ, or a combination

4 eggs

2 cups milk

Lightly butter a 1-quart baking dish.

Preheat the oven to 325 degrees F. Place in the oven a pan of water large enough to hold the 1-quart dish. Allow it to heat while preparing the pudding.

In a food processor, using the metal blade, finely chop the broccoli. Add the butter, seasonings, and oat bran or wheat germ. Blend to combine the ingredients. Add the eggs and run the machine for 8 seconds, scraping down the sides as needed. With the machine running, pour 1 cup of the milk through the feed tube and continue blending for 3 more seconds.

Pour the mixture into the prepared baking dish. Return the bowl and blade to the food processor base and add the remaining milk. Turn the machine on and off twice. (This will mix the milk with the particles of the batter that cling to the bowl and blade. It also contributes to the formation of the tasty pudding layer.) Pour over the mixture in the baking dish and stir gently until well mixed.

Carefully place the baking dish in the preheated water bath and bake for 60 minutes or until a knife inserted into the center comes out clean.

Yield: 4 to 6 servings

Carrot Pudding

This kugel is the stuff of dreams. The custardy texture is reminiscent of whipped cream; the subtle but intriguing flavor, which only hints at the vegetable from which it is made, may well tempt you to "eat the whole thing." What a lovely way to enrich your life with many immune-building carotenoids.

4 medium-size carrots, cut into 1-inch lengths, cooked and drained

3 small scallions

1 tablespoon butter, melted, **or oil**

½ teaspoon salt-free herbal seasoning

¼ teaspoon pepper

¼ teaspoon crushed dried thyme

⅓ cup oat bran or wheat germ, or a combination

4 large eggs

2 cups milk

Follow the directions for Broccoli Pudding *(see page 66)*, substituting the carrots and scallions for the broccoli.

Yield: 4 to 6 servings

SPINACH PUDDING

What little fat there is in spinach is of the Omega-3 variety, the same artery-cleansing type you get in fish.

Spinach is also high in fiber and vitamin E for extra protection against cancer and for cardiovascular health.

¼ **pound spinach**, cooked, drained, and squeezed dry in paper towels (frozen spinach may be used)

1 **tablespoon butter**, melted

1½ **tablespoons lemon juice**

¼ **teaspoon nutmeg**

½ **teaspoon salt-free herbal seasoning**

⅛ **teaspoon pepper**

⅓ **cup oat bran or wheat germ**, or a combination of the two

4 **large eggs**

2 **cups milk**

Follow the directions for Broccoli Pudding *(see page 66)*, substituting the spinach for the broccoli.

Yield: 4 to 6 servings

CREAMY CARAWAY CABBAGE

When selecting a head of cabbage, choose one with leaves that are tight to the head. It will bring crisp freshness to this recipe, which is a pleasant blend of sweet and tart, a lovely accompaniment for a dairy meal.

1 **small head of cabbage**

2 **tablespoons butter**

1 **teaspoon herbal seasoning**

1 **garlic clove**, minced

1 **tablespoon caraway seeds**

1 **teaspoon honey**

1 **tablespoon vinegar**, or to taste

½ **cup plain yogurt**

Trim and shred the cabbage coarsely using a sharp knife or the food processor. In a skillet, melt the butter. Add the shredded cabbage, herbal seasoning, and garlic. Stir well. Cover the skillet tightly and steam for 10 minutes.

Remove the cover and add the caraway seeds, honey, and vinegar. Mix well, then stir in the yogurt. Heat gently but do not boil. Serve immediately.

Yield: 4 servings

Asparagus, Carrots, and Pineapple

A lovely marriage of flavors and nutrients.

1 can (13½ ounces) **unsweetened pineapple chunks with juice**

Water

2 cups sliced carrots

Freshly ground pepper to taste

½ **pound asparagus,** sliced into 1-inch lengths

A few gratings of nutmeg

Drain the pineapple juice into a glass measuring cup; reserve the pineapple chunks.

Add water to the juice to make 1 cup. Pour into a medium-size saucepan. Add the carrots and pepper. Cook for about 10 minutes, until the carrots are crisp-tender. Add the asparagus and cook until tender—about 5 more minutes.

Stir in the reserved pineapple chunks and cook long enough to heat through. Sprinkle with nutmeg.

Yield: 6 servings

BROCCOLI AND ONIONS IN CHEESE SAUCE

Broccoli is practically a health prescription with its big bag of carotene, vitamin C, folic acid, bone-building boron, calcium, and fiber. This delicious dish is made the new way—in the microwave.

1 bunch broccoli, washed and cut; **or 1 package** (10 ounces) **frozen cut broccoli**

1 medium onion, cut into wedges

1 tablespoon water

½ cup milk

4 tablespoons Neufchâtel or yogurt cheese *(see index for recipe)*

1 teaspoon arrowroot starch or cornstarch

½ teaspoon lemon juice

½ teaspoon crushed dried basil

½ teaspoon crushed dried oregano

In a microwave-safe 1½-quart casserole, combine the broccoli, onion, and water. Microwave on high for 4 to 6 minutes or until the broccoli is crisp-tender. Drain.

In a small microwave-safe bowl, using a wire whisk, combine the milk, cheese, starch, lemon juice, basil, and oregano. Microwave on high, uncovered, for 2 to 3 minutes or until the sauce thickens. Pour the hot cheese sauce over the cooked broccoli.

Yield: 4 servings

Brussels Sprouts with Mustard Sauce

1 pound brussels sprouts

1½ tablespoons butter or olive oil

1 tablespoon lemon juice

1½ teaspoons prepared mustard, preferably coarse-grained

Wash the sprouts and trim off the bottoms. Steam for about 10 minutes.

In a microwave-safe dish or in a heatproof serving dish, melt or soften the butter. Stir in the lemon juice and mustard.

When the sprouts are crisp-tender, drain them and stir into the mustard mixture, coating well.

Yield: 4 servings

Like the other members of the crucifer family, brussels sprouts contain a substance called indoles, which have been shown to inhibit cancer. They provide vitamin C, vitamin A, and riboflavin—all of which are antioxidants, which quench those destructive free radicals.

This queen of the cabbage family also provides potassium, iron, and fiber. Brussels sprouts are very low in sodium and are a weight-watcher's delight—only 55 calories in a cup.

In spite of their value as a health protector, I confess that I was never able to "sell" them to my family until I discovered this zesty way to prepare them.

CREAM OF CAULIFLOWER SOUP WITH SUNFLOWER SEEDS

Another tasty member of the crucifer family, cauliflower is among the vegetables recognized as a cancer preventer by the Committee on Diet, Nutrition and Cancer of the National Academy of Sciences.

Sunflower seeds provide a whole bag of nutrients and a pleasant crunch to this deliciously satisfying soup.

½ head of a medium-size cauliflower

2 cups vegetable broth or water

1 clove garlic, minced

Dash of cayenne pepper

1 tablespoon grated Parmesan cheese

¼ cup lowfat plain yogurt

4 teaspoons toasted sunflower seeds

Sprinkle of Lemon Pepper
(recipe follows)

In a bowl or food processor, chop the cauliflower fine. Place the chopped cauliflower in a 2-quart microwave-safe bowl. Add the broth or water, garlic, and cayenne pepper. Cover the bowl and microwave on high for 2 to 4 minutes, until hot. Stir in the cheese and yogurt.

To serve, pour the soup into 4 bowls and sprinkle each with a teaspoon of sunflower seeds and a little lemon pepper.

Yield: 4 servings

LEMON PEPPER

2 tablespoons grated lemon peel

1 tablespoon coarsely ground pepper

Combine the ingredients and the seasoning is ready to use.

Yield: 3 tablespoons

BAKED RUTABAGA AND SWEET POTATOES

1 pound rutabaga, peeled, quartered, and thinly sliced

1 onion, thinly sliced

2 cloves garlic, minced

1 tablespoon olive or canola oil

1 teaspoon herbal seasoning

Freshly ground pepper to taste

1½ pounds unpeeled sweet potatoes, scrubbed and cut into bite-size chunks

In a 2-quart casserole, bring 1 quart of water to a boil. Add the rutabaga and cook for 3 minutes. Drain well.

In a skillet, soften the onion and garlic in the oil and season with the herbal seasoning and freshly ground pepper. Spread a third of the onion mixture over the bottom of a 2-quart casserole. Top with half the sweet potatoes and half the rutabaga, followed by another third of the onion mixture, the remaining sweet potatoes and rutabaga, and the rest of the onion mixture, along with any seasonings or oil clinging to the skillet.

Cover and bake at 350 degrees F. for 1 hour or until the vegetables are soft and their flavors blended.

Yield: 4 to 5 servings

Rutabaga, an honorable member of the crucifer family, is another cancer-fighting giant. Don't pass it up. Use it raw in your salad; put it in chicken soup and vegetable soup; combine it, cooked, with mashed potatoes; and combine it with sweet potatoes, a beta carotene wonder-worker that has been shown to protect against tumor growth.

Both rutabaga and sweet potatoes are high in potassium and fiber and are extremely low in calories—29 for a half-cup of cooked rutabaga and only 118 for a medium-size sweet potato. To make this dish even sweeter, consider that it has practically no fat and very little sodium—great for your blood pressure and your waistline.

EGGPLANT MANICOTTI

The shiny purple eggplant is lovingly known as Mediterranean "medicine." No wonder. It is low in fat, sodium, and calories but high in fiber and potassium. Some studies have suggested that eggplant itself, with more fiber than oat bran, can help lower cholesterol. Stuffed into manicotti shells and covered with spaghetti sauce and cheese, it creates a dish of "medicine" you will savor with pleasure.

1 package (8 ounces) **manicotti shells** (16 shells)

2 tablespoons olive or canola oil

1 large garlic clove, thinly sliced

1 medium-size eggplant (about 1 pound), chopped

½ cup chopped onion

½ cup water

1 jar (32 ounces) **spaghetti sauce**

½ pound part-skim mozzarella cheese, shredded

1 cup ricotta, cottage, farmer, or pot cheese

¾ cup dried whole-grain bread crumbs

2 eggs

½ teaspoon Italian seasoning

⅛ teaspoon freshly ground pepper

Cook the manicotti shells *al dente,* according to package directions. Drain. In a 12-inch skillet, over medium heat, heat the oil, then cook the garlic until just brown. Discard the garlic. In the remaining oil in the skillet, cook the eggplant and onion for 5 minutes, stirring frequently. Add water, cover, and cook for 10 minutes or until tender. Remove from the heat and cool the mixture slightly.

Preheat the oven to 375 degrees F.

In a 13 x 9–inch baking dish, spread half the spaghetti sauce, then sprinkle on half of the mozzarella cheese.

In another bowl, combine the ricotta or other cheese, bread crumbs, eggs, and the seasonings.

Mix well, then add the cooked eggplant. Using a spoon, fill each manicotti shell with 2 heaping tablespoons of the mixture.

Arrange the filled manicotti shells in a single layer in the baking dish.

Pour the remaining spaghetti sauce over the shells; sprinkle with the remaining mozzarella cheese. Cover the dish with foil and bake for 20 minutes. Remove the foil and bake for 10 minutes longer or until mixture is hot and bubbly.

Yield: 6 servings

BANANA AND EGGPLANT

A happy marriage of flavors and nutrients that is surprisingly delicious. The mellow flavor of the banana is a perfect counterpart to the zesty flavors of the other ingredients. It goes great with a fish or meat meal, or served with brown rice for a vegetarian delight.

2 tablespoons olive or canola oil

1 medium-size eggplant, peeled and cubed

1 medium-size onion, sliced

3 medium-size bananas, sliced

1 can (15 ounces) **tomato sauce**

1 teaspoon crushed dried marjoram

Freshly ground pepper and herbal seasoning to taste

Heat the oil in a skillet. Add the eggplant and onion and sauté until golden. Add the bananas, tomato sauce, and seasonings. Simmer the mixture until the eggplant is soft, about 10 minutes.

Yield: 4 to 6 servings

BROCCOLI-STUFFED POTATOES

You'll never again need to shtup the kids to eat their broccoli. The first time I served these, one of my grandchildren, a former broccoli scorner, gave them his highest recommendation when he said, "These are better than pizza!"

3 large baked potatoes

½ head of broccoli, steamed until crisp-tender then chopped

¼ cup milk

¾ cup grated part-skim mozzarella cheese

1 tablespoon unsalted butter

⅛ teaspoon freshly ground pepper

1 teaspoon herbal seasoning

Slice each of the baked potatoes in half and scoop the insides into a bowl with the chopped broccoli. Reserve the potato shells.

To the broccoli and potato mixture, add the milk, ½ cup of the cheese, the butter, and the seasonings. Mash all together or combine the ingredients in the food processor and process briefly.

Stuff the mixture into the potato skins and sprinkle with the remaining cheese. Line up the stuffed spuds in a baking dish and place in a 400-degree F. oven for about 10 minutes.

Yield: 6 servings

Spinach with Wheat Germ, Nuts, and Raisins

1 pound spinach, washed and stems removed (use the stems in vegetable broth)

1 tablespoon canola or olive oil

2 cloves garlic, minced

Pinch of cayenne pepper

¼ cup raisins

¼ cup sunflower seeds or chopped walnuts

¼ cup wheat germ

¼ cup grated Parmesan cheese

Immerse the washed spinach in boiling water, then drain immediately. Chop coarsely and reserve.

Heat the oil in large skillet. Add the garlic and cayenne. Sauté for about a minute. Stir in the raisins and sunflower seeds or walnuts. Mix the skillet mixture into the spinach. Transfer to a 1-quart casserole.

Combine the wheat germ and the cheese. Sprinkle this mixture over the top of the casserole and broil until the cheese is lightly browned, about 2 minutes.

Yield: 4 servings

I classify the deep green leaves of spinach as a healthy pleasure. You can nibble on a half cup of crisp raw spinach and consume only 6 calories. If you cook it first, you'll get 21 calories in a half-cup.

But look what you get with those meager calories: vitamin E, a powerful antioxidant for extra protection against the scourge of cancer and heart disease, and beta carotene, another powerful antioxidant which acts as a health guardian. And let's not forget the pleasure *you will discover when you try this recipe.*

6

Healthy Food Adds to the Joy of Passover

Passover is a celebration of memories—not only the memory of making bricks without straw, the ten plagues, Miriam's song of jubilation after the crossing of the Sea of Reeds, but memories of the Passovers of our childhood: the fun of the nuts-against-the-wall game while the heavenly aromas from the kitchen made our tastebuds do a hora.

Picture this: The whole house is scrubbed from top to bottom; freshly-starched curtains hang from the windows like bridal veils; our venerable ancestors smile out of picture frames that shine with a new coat of golden luster; we kids are freshly bathed and dressed in brand new clothes; everybody's eyes are twinkling, reflecting all the sparkling surfaces of polished wood, stove, and samovar. Everything is *freilach* (joyful).

I remember feeling sorry for my non-Jewish friends because they didn't have the joy and excitement of Passover. They thought we were deprived because we couldn't have bread. Can you imagine? Who needs bread when there are knaidlach (matzo balls) in the soup; charoset, kugels, bitter herbs, and sweet wine on the table; and memories, hopes, and family togetherness? For, in spite of the restrictions against bread, flour, legumes, yeast, and anything which would, with the addition of water, begin to ferment, the foods of Passover have a very special *Pesachdik tam* (Passover flavor).

However, to keep indigestion from marring the joy of the holiday, we must seek other sources for the nutrients and fiber which are usually provided by whole-grain flour, wheat germ, and bran, foods which are not on the Passover menu.

To make your Passover dishes more wholesome and high in fiber, use kosher-for-Passover whole-wheat matzo at the table, in kugels, and in matzo brei. Until your family becomes accustomed to the coarser texture of the whole wheat, mix some white matzo with the whole wheat.

Make your own whole-wheat matzo meal by whizzing some whole wheat matzo in a blender or food processor. And make your own whole-grain farfel by breaking whole-wheat matzos into small pieces. Get the children to do the breaking. They love to break things, and they get a kick out of eating the things they've had a hand in.

The following recipes will bring extra nutritional values and exciting new tastes to your Passover table.

PASSOVER NOODLES

Fortunately, potato starch is kosher for Passover. It is far more wholesome than cornstarch, which is ultra-refined and contributes calories without nutrients. Potato starch, on the other hand, contributes lots of potassium, is a fairly good source of iron and calcium, and provides vitamin C and some of the B vitamins, particularly niacin, which has been found to lower cholesterol levels.

6 eggs
¼ **teaspoon salt** (optional)
¾ **cup potato starch**
Peanut oil

In a mixing bowl or food processor, blend together the eggs and salt, then blend in the potato starch.

Lightly grease a frying pan with peanut oil. Preheat the pan over medium heat then pour a small amount of the mixture into the pan; immediately pour off excess batter. Cook lightly on both sides, but do not brown. Remove and let cool. When all the batter has been used up, roll each pancake individually and slice thin into noodles. Allow to dry out and store in a tightly-sealed container until ready to use. Very nice in chicken soup.

You can also use these pancakes, cooked on one side only, as blintz blankets.

Yield: approximately 8 ounces

Farfel Chicken Casserole

1 to 2 tablespoons chicken fat or peanut oil

1 large onion, diced

1 cup chicken soup

1 cup vegetable juice, stock, or water

2 cups cooked chicken, cut up

2 cups cooked sliced carrots or other vegetable

1 cup diced celery

1½ cups matzo farfel (whole-wheat matzo broken into farfel)

Freshly ground pepper and paprika

In a large saucepan, heat the chicken fat or oil. Add the onion and sauté until transparent but not yet browned. Add the chicken soup and vegetable juice, stock, or water to make a sauce.

Arrange the chicken, vegetables, matzo farfel, and the sauce in alternate layers in a 2-quart casserole. Season to taste with a bit of pepper and paprika.

Cover and bake in a preheated 350-degree F. oven for about 30 minutes.

Yield: 6 to 8 servings

Chicken is high in protein, low in fat, low in calories, and is easily digested. It is also an excellent source of iron, potassium, calcium, vitamin A, and the B vitamins. Chicken provides no carbohydrate and no fiber, both of which are amply supplied in the whole-wheat matzo farfel and the vegetables called for in this recipe. This casserole is so tasty, it's nice to know your body is enjoying it as much as your palate.

PASSOVER PUFFS

These puffs made with whole-wheat matzo provide a high-protein, nutrient-rich "overcoat" for many delicious fillings. Try the filling below and create other fillings to suit your taste.

1 cup boiling water

⅓ cup peanut oil

½ teaspoon salt or herbal seasoning

1 cup cake meal (whole-wheat matzo ground to a powder in a blender or food processor)

4 eggs

In a saucepan, combine the water, oil, and seasoning. Bring to a slow boil and reduce the heat. Add the cake meal all at once. Stir vigorously over low heat until the mixture forms a ball and leaves the sides of the pan. Remove from the heat. Add the unbeaten eggs one at a time, beating very thoroughly after each addition, until the mixture is smooth and thick.

Drop by the heaping tablespoonful, about 2 inches apart, onto an oiled or parchment-lined cookie sheet.

Bake in a preheated 400-degree F. oven for about 40 minutes, until puffed and golden brown. (Do not open the oven door during the early part of the baking period.) Remove the golden brown puffs from the oven and transfer to a rack. When the puffs are cool, cut off the tops and fill with chicken, tuna, mixed vegetables, a dessert filling—or the filling of your choice.

Yield: 12 to 16 puffs

CHICKEN SALAD FILLING FOR PUFFS:

1 cup diced cooked chicken

⅓ cup chopped celery

½ cup presoaked raisins, chopped apple, or pineapple cubes

½ cup slivered almonds or chopped cashews

3 tablespoons reduced-fat mayonnaise

In a medium-size bowl, combine the chicken, celery, fruit of your choice, and nuts. Add the mayonnaise and mix to blend.

Yield: 1½ cups, enough to fill 6 large or 12 small puffs quite generously

TUNA SALAD FILLING FOR PUFFS:

1 can (7 ounces) **tuna,** drained

1 stalk celery, chopped

1 medium-size carrot, grated

3 tablespoons reduced-fat mayonnaise

2 tablespoons lemon juice

Pinch each of dill weed, paprika, and dried oregano

In a medium-size bowl, combine all the ingredients.

Yield: a little over 1 cup, enough for 6 large or 12 small puffs

CUSTARD FILLING FOR PUFFS (CREAM PUFFS):

⅓ cup potato starch

1⅓ cups milk

2 egg yolks

2 tablespoons honey

1 teaspoon vanilla extract

In a small bowl, dissolve the potato starch in ⅓ cup of the milk. In the top part of a double boiler, heat the remaining cup of milk to a simmer. Mix the dissolved potato starch into the simmering milk and cook until thickened, stirring constantly—about 1 minute.

Beat the egg yolks with the honey. Whisk a little of the hot mixture into the egg mixture, then stir this into the remaining hot milk mixture. Cook for about 1 minute, stirring constantly to prevent lumps from forming. Add the vanilla, pour into a bowl and chill.

Yield: 1½ cups, enough to fill 6 large or 12 small puffs

APPLE-MATZO KUGEL

Enjoy a cinnamony apple flavor in every bite of this moist kugel. It's pareve, so you can serve it at either a meat or dairy meal.

4 matzos (preferably whole-wheat)

3 eggs, well beaten

⅓ cup honey

1 teaspoon ground cinnamon

Pinch of grated nutmeg

½ cup chopped walnuts, pecans, or sunflower seeds

2 large unpeeled apples, scrubbed and chopped

½ cup raisins

Break the matzos in ½-inch pieces. Place in a bowl and soak in water until soft. Drain but do not squeeze dry.

In a separate bowl, beat the eggs with the honey;

add the spices. Stir in the chopped nuts, chopped apple, soaked matzos, and the raisins.

Turn into a lightly oiled 6 x 10–inch baking dish. Bake in a preheated 350-degree F. oven for 45 minutes or until lightly browned.

Yield: 6 to 8 servings

Matzo Brei

A great breakfast, lunch, or supper during Passover. Make it with whole-wheat matzo and provide a good supply of pantothenic acid, vitamin E (the anti-stress vitamin, an important anti-oxidant), and fiber, all of which are in short supply in the Passover diet.

8 whole-wheat matzos

3 to 4 cups boiling water

4 eggs, lightly beaten

Salt or herbal seasoning and ground pepper to taste

Butter or oil for frying

Break the matzos into 2-inch squares. Place in a large bowl or pot. Pour boiling water over the matzo pieces and drain immediately through a colander. The pieces should be only slightly moistened, so they will absorb the egg. Return the matzo to the bowl. Add the beaten egg and seasonings. Toss with a fork until all pieces are coated.

In a heavy 10- to 12-inch skillet, heat the butter or oil until bubbly but not browned. Pour the matzo mixture into the pan and fry over medium heat. When the underside begins to brown, turn the entire matzo brei with a spatula. If it breaks, turn it in sections. Turn until all sides are golden. It doesn't matter if the matzo brei crumbles. These little nuggets add an extra dimension to the enjoyment of the dish. Taste-check and adapt the seasoning. It will take about 10 minutes to complete the frying.

Excellent with cottage cheese or yogurt.

Yield: 4 to 6 servings

PASSOVER GRANOLA

A welcome change from fried matzo for breakfast, this granola is deliciously crunchy and flavorful. It can also be used as a dessert topping and as an unbaked pie crust.

6 whole-wheat matzos broken into ½-inch pieces

2 cups unsweetened shredded coconut

1 cup sunflower seeds

½ cup chopped cashews or walnuts

½ teaspoon ground cinnamon

1 cup fruit juice or 1 cup water sweetened with 2 tablespoons honey

½ cup slivered almonds

Raisins, dates, prunes, or dried figs

In a large bowl, combine the matzo pieces with the rest of the dry ingredients except for the slivered almonds and the dried fruit. Mix well. Drizzle the fruit juice or the honeyed water over all a little at a time, mixing it through.

Preheat the oven to 225 degrees F. Spread the mixture over 2 cookie sheets that have been lightly greased or lined with parchment paper. Bake for 1 hour, stirring occasionally. Add the almonds and bake for another 15 minutes or until the mixture is dry and toasty brown. Turn off the oven and let the mixture cool in the oven. You can add dried fruit at this point or at serving time.

Store in tightly-covered containers (Mason jars are good) in the refrigerator or freezer. Good with hot or cold milk or with yogurt.

MICROWAVE METHOD:

Follow the above instructions for preparing the moistened mixture. Spread parchment paper on the floor of the microwave oven. Spread half of the moistened mixture on the parchment paper. Microcook uncovered, on medium power, for 5 minutes. Add the slivered almonds and microcook for another minute. Leave the mixture in the oven for about 5 minutes, until thoroughly dry and crisp. Repeat the procedure with the other half of the mixture.

Yield: 2 quarts, 16 to 20 servings

Low-Fat, Low-Calorie Passover Kishke

Seconds on the kishke? Why not? It's wholesome, low in fat and calories, and tastes like the real thing—without the heartburn.

2 stalks celery with leaves

1 large carrot, scrubbed and chunked

1 large onion, quartered

1 egg

¼ cup peanut oil

½ teaspoon herbal seasoning

¼ cup poppy seeds

1¼ cups matzo cake meal (preferably whole-grain)

Paprika to taste

Whiz the vegetables, egg, oil, seasoning, and poppy seeds in a blender or food processor. Combine this mixture with the cake meal and paprika.

Spoon half this mixture onto a sheet of parchment paper. Shape into a roll similar to a traditional kishke. Roll it securely, then twist the ends of the paper. Repeat with the other half of the mixture. Transfer the rolls to a cookie sheet or baking dish and bake in a preheated 350-degree F. oven for 1 hour. This kishke can be frozen before or after baking.

Yield: 2 kishke rolls

POTATO DUMPLINGS

These delicious knaidlach can be cooked in a carrot tsimmes, making the dish a complete meal, or it can be shaped into small balls and dropped into boiling water and cooked for an hour, then drained and served in soup or as a dumpling in a meat stew or fricassee.

3 large unpeeled potatoes, well scrubbed
1 cooked potato (optional)
2 eggs
⅓ cup oat bran or matzo meal
1 tablespoon chicken fat or olive oil
½ teaspoon salt (optional)
Dash of freshly ground black pepper
Dash of ground cinnamon

In the food processor, using the steel blade, grate the unpeeled potatoes. Add the cooked potato if you have one, the eggs, oat bran or matzo meal, the fat or oil, and the seasonings. Process to combine the ingredients. The mixture should be just firm enough to shape. If it is too soft, add a little more oat bran or matzo meal.

If you plan to cook the mixture in a tsimmes (use the Carrot Tsimmes recipe on page 106, but substitute potato starch for the arrowroot), form into 1 or 2 large oval dumplings and place them carefully in the center of the raw vegetables.

Yield: 20 dumplings, 8 to 10 servings

Faron Schonfeld's Banana Ice Cream

A Passover treat that's delicious every day of the year. When I demonstrated this dessert at a Passover workshop for confirmation class at Temple Beth El, in Allentown, Pennsylvania, Faron, an upperclassman, intrigued by the lovely flavor and ease of the preparation, developed many variations on the original theme, then made copies of the recipe to distribute to family and friends.

2 or 3 ripe bananas, cut into chunks and frozen

That's all you need for the basic recipe. All the rest is embellishment. Be adventurous and try them all:

fresh fruit; frozen fruit; carob syrup; sunflower or pumpkin seeds; chopped almonds, walnuts, or pecans—or soy nuts, lightly toasted

Freeze the chunked bananas for at least an hour. Remove from the freezer about 5 minutes before using. Place the bananas in the food processor and whiz for 20 to 40 seconds, or until they form a thick consistency similar to ice cream.

Add any toppings to enhance the flavor—including kosher-for-Passover chocolate chips.

Your dessert is ready! Enjoy! (Faron's words.)

Yield: 4 to 6 servings, depending on whether those enjoying are teenagers or adults

CHAROSET

This delicious sweet-tart mixture of fruit and nuts is served at the Seder to represent the mortar used to make bricks for Pharaoh. It is the morsel of sweetness meant to lighten the burden of bitter events.

2 unpeeled red apples, scrubbed and grated

½ cup chopped walnuts

1 teaspoon honey

Grated rind of 1 lemon

1 teaspoon ground cinnamon

2 tablespoons sweet red wine (approximately)

In a small bowl, combine the grated apples, nuts, honey, lemon rind, and cinnamon. Add only enough wine to bind the mixture. Taste-check for a good blend of sweet, sour, and crunch.

Yield: approximately 1 cup

MOCK OATMEAL COOKIES

These crunchy cookies, loaded with nuts and raisins, fill a real need for a nutritious Passover snack food.

¾ cup honey

⅓ cup peanut oil

4 eggs

2 cups whole-wheat matzo meal

2 cups whole-wheat matzo farfel

1 cup raisins

1 cup chopped walnuts

1 teaspoon ground cinnamon

In large mixing bowl or food processor, blend the honey, oil, and eggs. Add the remaining ingredients. Mix well. Drop by the teaspoonful onto a cookie sheet greased with peanut oil or butter, or lined with parchment paper. Bake in a preheated 325-degree F. oven for 20 to 25 minutes.

Yield: 4 dozen cookies

Delicious Passover Foods for Those on Special Diets

While many of us anticipate the joy of kugels, knaidlach, sponge cakes, and matzo brei, there are those among us who cannot tolerate eggs, wheat, salt, or sugar. What's there for them to eat on Passover?

Plenty. Go creative with vegetables, fruits, nuts, and raisins. For those who can't eat eggs, skip the matzo brei and serve Passover granola with milk or yogurt. If they can't handle eggs or dairy products, serve the granola with fruit juice.

For those who can't handle wheat, make a delicious carrot coconut cake.

SWEET POTATO AND CARROT RING

No eggs, no salt, no meat; high in the antioxidants beta carotene (as well as many other valuable carotenoids) and vitamin A; and containing many minerals and much fiber.

2 medium-size onions, chopped
1 tablespoon olive or canola oil
3 large carrots, cooked
3 large sweet potatoes, cooked
⅓ cup orange juice
1 tablespoon grated orange rind
1 tablespoon honey
4 tablespoons chopped or slivered almonds

In a medium-size skillet, lightly sauté the onions in the oil. Mash the carrots and sweet potatoes with a fork or whiz in a food processor. Stir in the sautéed onions, orange juice, orange rind, and honey. Beat until fluffy, then pile into a greased ring mold, top with the almonds, and bake in a preheated 350-degree F. oven for about 20 minutes.

Yield: 6 to 8 servings

CARROT COCONUT CAKE

Moist, kosher for Passover, and rich in vitamin A, magnesium, potassium, and fiber. What more could you ask?

1 cup grated raw carrot
¾ cup coconut crumbs
¾ cup honey or maple syrup
1 teaspoon vanilla extract
6 eggs, separated
1 cup ground raw cashews
3 teaspoons potato starch

In a large bowl, blend the carrot, coconut crumbs, and honey or syrup. Add the vanilla and blend. In a separate bowl, beat the egg yolks to a creamy consistency. Fold the egg yolks into the carrot-coconut mixture and let it stand in the refrigerator for 1 hour, or until it has soaked up the moisture. Add the ground cashews and blend.

In another bowl, beat the egg whites until stiff. Sprinkle the potato starch over them and mix it in. Fold the egg white mixture into the carrot-coconut mixture. Make two 9-inch layers or pour the mixture into a bundt pan. Bake in a preheated 400-degree F. oven for 10 minutes, then reduce the temperature to 350 degrees F. and bake for an additional 20 to 30 minutes or until the cake shows signs of leaving the sides of the pan. Cool on a wire rack.

Yield: 1 cake

7

Delicious Dairy Dishes for Shavuot

ne of the most joyful of festivals, Shavuot commemorates the Giving of the Law, the birthday of Moses having received the Torah on Mount Sinai.

Shavuot is also an agricultural festival celebrating the end of the barley harvest and the offering of the first fruits in the Temple. In observance of the agricultural aspects of the festival, it is customary to fill the house with freshly-cut greens and flowers.

In many synagogues, Confirmation services are observed on Shavuot. It is deemed fitting that boys and girls be confirmed in their Jewish faith on the anniversary of the day when their forefathers received the Law and were confirmed in their faith. It is also customary to herald the advent of Shavuot with an all-night vigil devoted to the study of Torah, with refreshment breaks for cheesecake and coffee.

Dairy dishes are served during this joyous festival because the Torah is said to be "as nutritious as milk and as sweet as honey." Cheese blintzes are particularly traditional because when two blintzes are placed side by side, they resemble the two tablets of the Law.

Though they taste sinfully rich, blintzes can be low on the calorie scale, rich in complex carbohydrates and a good source of fiber.

BLINTZES

Nothing says "welcome to our table" like a plateful of snugly-wrapped blintzes (crêpes), each tender crust enfolding a tasty filling of cheese, potatoes, or fruit. But, most blintz recipes call for butter in the batter and more butter in the frying pan. Who needs all that fat? Believe me, you can make delicious blintzes without it. The only butter you need is a little smidgen to grease the pan in which you fry or bake them.

VERY THIN BLINTZ BLANKETS:

2 eggs plus 1 egg white (retain the yolk for the filling)

1 cup water

1 cup whole-wheat pastry flour

In a blender or food processor, blend together the eggs, water, and flour until smooth. Transfer to a bowl and refrigerate for 2 hours or overnight before using.

To prepare the blintz blankets, heat a 6- or 7-inch nonstick skillet until a few drops of water sprinkled on it do a lively dance. If the pan has not been seasoned, coat lightly with nonstick spray.

Pour ¼ cup of batter into the skillet. Tilt the pan to coat the bottom evenly. Immediately pour excess batter back into the batter bowl.

Cook over medium heat until lightly browned. Bump the bletl (blintz blanket) onto a tea towel. Fold the towel over it to prevent it from drying out. Repeat the process until the batter is used up, stacking the bletlach on the tea towel and covering with the towel. They will not stick together.

Yield: about 20 very thin bletlach

ASSEMBLING THE BLINTZES:

Use the cheese filling in the recipe that follows or create blueberry-cheese filling by adding a tablespoon of blueberries to the cheese filling for each blintz. Or use a potato or kasha filling or try a mixture of stir-fried vegetables cut into very small pieces and nicely seasoned. Since the bletlach are pareve, you can also make tasty fleishig blintzes.

The filled blintzes can be sautéed in a lightly greased skillet or baked in a single layer in a greased baking dish at 350 degrees F. for 15 minutes or until golden. (Baking is more healthful than frying.)

Note: You can make any kind of blintz in advance and refrigerate or freeze before the frying or baking stage. It's a good idea to bring them to room temperature before cooking.

CHEESE FILLING:

1 pound cottage cheese, drained

4 ounces Neufchâtel cream cheese (calorie-reduced)

1 egg yolk

2 teaspoons honey

1 teaspoon vanilla extract

Dash of ground cinnamon

¼ teaspoon grated lemon rind

In a mixing bowl or food processor, blend all ingredients and you've got it made. Place a tablespoon of filling just below the center of each bletl. Fold both sides over the filling and roll, enclosing the filling.

Yield: enough filling for 20 blintzes

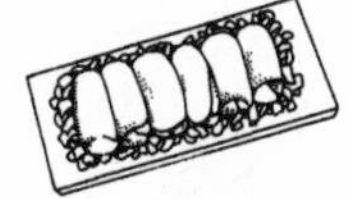

BLINTZ MUFFINS

These are quick and easy and great for snacks and lunch boxes.

3 eggs

1 pound cottage cheese

3 tablespoons sour cream or yogurt

3 tablespoons unsalted butter

2 tablespoons honey, or to taste

1 teaspoon vanilla extract

½ cup whole-wheat pastry flour

2 teaspoons baking powder

½ teaspoon ground cinnamon

In a mixing bowl or food processor, combine the eggs, cheese, sour cream or yogurt, butter, honey, and vanilla. Process briefly to blend the ingredients.

In another bowl, combine the flour, baking powder, and cinnamon. Add this mixture to the cheese mixture and process only until no flour is visible.

Grease with butter or oil, or shpritz with cooking spray, 12 regular-size muffin cups. Fill and bake in a preheated 350-degree F. oven for 25 minutes. Serve the muffins piping hot or at room temperature.

Yield: 12 muffins

Blintz Loaf

1 pound cottage cheese, drained
3 ounces Neufchâtel cream cheese
3 eggs
½ teaspoon lemon juice
½ teaspoon vanilla extract
½ cup whole-wheat pastry flour
½ teaspoon baking powder
2 tablespoons honey, or to taste
Ground cinnamon

As a change from individual blintzes, try this delicious loaf. A wonderful addition to a buffet table.

In a mixing bowl or food processor, combine the cheeses and eggs. Add the lemon juice, vanilla, flour, baking powder, and honey. Mix or process until the ingredients are well combined.

Pour the mixture into a buttered 8 x 8–inch baking pan. Dust with cinnamon. Bake in a preheated 325-degree F. oven for 40 to 50 minutes or until nicely browned. Serve hot or cold with yogurt or a fruit sauce.

Yield: 6 to 8 servings

PINEAPPLE NOODLE KUGEL

For more nutrients and more fiber, make this kugel with whole-wheat noodles. They cook up almost white and have a more robust, satisfying flavor. If you chose to use white noodles, add 3 tablespoons of wheat germ to the ingredients.

8 ounces medium noodles

1 pound cottage cheese

1 cup sour cream or yogurt, or half of each

2 tablespoons lecithin granules (optional)

1 cup milk

3 eggs, beaten

1 can (20 ounces) **crushed pineapple,** drained

¼ **cup honey** (or a little less)

4 tablespoons unsalted butter, melted

½ **cup raisins**

1 teaspoon vanilla extract

Ground cinnamon to taste

Boil the noodles in lightly salted water according to package directions. Drain.

Preheat the oven to 350 degrees F.

In a large bowl, combine all the ingredients, including the drained noodles. Pour into a well-buttered 11 x 14–inch baking dish. Bake for 1 hour or until the top is golden and crusty.

Yield: 8 to10 servings

Butternut Squash Casserole

This versatile, easy-to-prepare dish can be served hot or cold, as a main dish for a heart-healthy meatless meal or as a side dish for an elegant dinner party or a take-along buffet.

5 cups grated butternut squash
(about 1 pound)

Juice and grated rind of 1 lemon

1 cup raisins

10 dried apricots, diced

½ cup chopped pitted prunes

1 large apple, washed and diced

1½ cups cottage cheese

3 tablespoons plain yogurt or sour cream
(if you're not counting calories)

2 teaspoons ground cinnamon

⅛ teaspoon grated nutmeg

1 egg

½ cup chopped walnuts

Combine the squash, lemon rind and juice. Spread 3 cups of this mixture in a 9 x 12 x 2–inch casserole that has been buttered or coated with nonstick baking spray.

In a small bowl, combine the raisins, apricots, prunes, and apple. Spread this mixture over the squash.

Combine the cottage cheese, yogurt or sour cream, cinnamon, nutmeg, and egg. Spread this mixture over the fruit mixture, then top with the remaining squash mixture. Sprinkle with the chopped walnuts and bake in a preheated 375-degree F. oven for 30 minutes or until deliciously golden.

Yield: 4 servings as a main dish, 8 as a side dish

MAPLE WALNUT CHEESECAKE

Devilishly good but calorie-reduced and rich in wholesome nutrients.

CRUST:

¼ cup wheat germ

¼ cup ground walnuts

¼ cup shredded coconut

FILLING:

3 cups ricotta cheese

⅓ cup maple syrup

3 eggs, separated

1 teaspoon vanilla extract

1 tablespoon lemon juice

2 tablespoons arrowroot starch or cornstarch

1 teaspoon cream of tartar

2 tablespoons maple syrup

Walnuts halves for garnish

To prepare the crust: Combine the wheat germ, walnuts, and coconut. Reserve 2 tablespoons of this mixture for garnish. Coat the sides of a well-buttered 9-inch springform pan with the dry mixture and spread the remaining mixture evenly over the bottom of the pan.

To prepare the filling: In a large mixing bowl or food processor, combine the ricotta and ⅓ cup of maple syrup. Process until light and fluffy. Add the egg yolks, vanilla, lemon juice, and starch.

In another bowl, beat the egg whites until soft peaks form. Add the cream of tartar and 2 tablespoons of maple syrup and beat until the egg whites are stiff. Fold the egg-white mixture into the cheese mixture, then pour into the prepared crust. Garnish with the reserved wheat germ mixture and the walnut halves.

Bake in a preheated 350-degree F. oven for 1 hour. Then turn off the heat but leave the cake in the oven until the oven is cool. Remove the cake from the oven and let it cool completely on a rack. Run a knife along the sides of the cake to release it from the rim. Carefully remove the rim. Similarly, loosen the bottom. Slide 2 large spatulas under the cake and transfer it to a serving platter. Chill.

Yield: 12 portions

Macaroon Raisin-Rum Cheesecake

Now's your chance to indulge in a sinfully delicious cheesecake without guilt. This one will not expand your waistline. It's made with ricotta cheese. If you don't have almond macaroons, use graham crackers or your own home-baked cookie crumbs.

1 cup dry almond macaroons, crushed
½ cup golden raisins
3 tablespoons dark Jamaican rum
1½ cups ricotta cheese
¼ cup honey
4 eggs, separated
1 teaspoon lemon juice
1 teaspoon lemon rind
1 teaspoon vanilla extract
¼ teaspoon almond extract

To prepare the crust: Coat a 9-inch springform pan with butter or nonstick baking spray. Reserve ¼ cup of the macaroon crumbs for topping. Dust the sides of pan with macaroon crumbs, then press the remaining crumbs firmly over bottom of the pan.

Preheat the oven to 300 degrees F.

To prepare the filling: Combine the raisins and rum in a small bowl and let stand. In another bowl or in a food processor, blend the cheese, honey, and egg yolks until smooth. Add the lemon juice and rind, then the vanilla and almond extracts. Mix to blend.

In another bowl, beat the egg whites until stiff but not dry. Fold the whites into the cheese mixture. Gently stir in the raisin and rum mixture. Pour into the prepared pan and sprinkle with the reserved ¼ cup of macaroon crumbs.

Bake the cheesecake in the preheated oven for 1 hour. Turn off the oven but leave the cake in the unopened oven for 2 hours. Then remove the cake from the oven and let it cool on a wire rack to room temperature. Refrigerate overnight.

Yield: 8 to 10 luscious servings

8

THE HIGH HOLIDAYS (Rich in Tradition and Nutrition)

On Rosh Hashana, the Jewish New Year, we traditionally eat foods that are sweet in taste and round in shape. The sweet foods—the apple dipped in honey, the honey cake, the carrot tsimmes—all imply a wish for a sweet and pleasant New Year. No sour or bitter foods are included in this holiday's menu. The round foods, such as the round *challot* (plural of challah), symbolize the wish for health and happiness without end.

For the meal before the Yom Kippur (Day of Atonement) fast, a favorite dish is kreplach. It is said that the meat symbolizes inflexible justice; the soft dough which covers it denotes compassion. Reflect on this the next time you bite into delicious kreplach—and ponder, too, on the many ways in which what we eat is woven into our stream of life.

Other dishes served at the pre-Yom Kippur meal should be bland, without spices or salt, to lessen the incidence of thirst during the fast.

After Yom Kippur, to break the fast, it is always good to start with something light, perhaps a fruit-and-yogurt preparation or an omelet with a hot beverage and whole-wheat toast, fruit juice, or soup. Pickled herring is much too salty to serve as a fast-breaker. This salt-load is dangerous for people with high blood pressure. Recipes for dishes to adorn your Yom Kippur night buffet table can be found throughout the book. You'll find them easily by consulting the index.

ROUND CHALLAH

Round challah is served on the High Holidays as a silent wish that our joy and good fortune will be without end in the coming year.

To make a round challah, follow the instructions for making challah dough in Chapter Seventeen, The Joy of Baking Bread. Divide the dough in half. Reserve an egg-size chunk of dough from each half.

Roll out each of the large portions of dough to resemble a rope about 16 inches long, tapering the ends. Coil each rope, tightly tucking the ends under. Place them on a cookie sheet or in round cake pans shpritzed with nonstick baking spray.

From the reserved balls of dough, delight your family by forming ladders (symbolic of one's reach up for guidance and of the hope that one's prayers may ascend on high), as follows:

For each ladder, form the dough into 2 thin strips for the sides and 4 thin strips for the rungs. Place one ladder on each challah and brush the ladders and the rest of the challah with egg wash (1 egg yolk beaten with 1 teaspoon water). Sprinkle with poppy or sesame seeds.

Cover the challot with a clean towel and allow to rise for about 2 hours or until double in bulk. Bake in a 375-degree F. oven for 30 to 35 minutes, until a tap on the bottom elicits a hollow sound. *Gut yomtov!*

Yield: 2 round challot

Farfel

1 egg

⅞ cup whole-wheat pastry flour

Pinch of herbal seasoning

These are noodle balls no larger than barley grains. Farfel, not to be confused with matzo farfel, which are pieces of broken-up matzo used on Passover, are usually served on Rosh Hashana because of their rounded form. When made from whole-wheat flour, they are a health-building food.

Combine the ingredients and knead into a hard ball. The dough will be stiff. Grate it on a fine grater and spread it out to dry thoroughly.

To cook, add to boiling water or drop into boiling soup. Cook for about 30 minutes. They take longer than most noodles.

Yield: approximately 1½ cups

Potato Knishes

A must for holiday meals. Our kids call these the "convertibles" because they have soft tops, unlike the knishes that are rolled in dough. These are much easier to prepare and very delicious.

6 potatoes, boiled and mashed

2 eggs, beaten (reserve 2 tablespoons)

Grieben or sautéed onion (quantities to taste)

Freshly ground pepper and herbal seasoning to taste

Blend together the potatoes, eggs, grieben or sautéed onion, and seasonings. Form into patties about ½-inch thick. Place on a cookie sheet

Nutritionally speaking, potatoes are high in vitamin C complex, a better vitamin C pattern than is found in citrus fruit because it contains the tyrosinase fraction, the organic copper blood-builder.

shpritzed with nonstick spray or chicken fat or canola oil. Brush the patties with the reserved egg. Bake in a preheated 375-degree F. oven for about 35 minutes, until brown and aromatic.

Yield: 12 knishes

CARROT TSIMMES

A carrot tsimmes expresses a wish for a sweet New Year, one rich in fulfillment and productivity. The Yiddish word for carrot is merin, *which also means "to increase, multiply."*

This tsimmes should do wonders for your complexion and for your health in general. Carrots are loaded with beta carotene

2 pounds meat (brust, flanken, or brisket)

1 bay leaf

Water or stock

2 medium-size onions, sliced

5 large carrots, preferably organic, scrubbed and chunked

2 large or 4 small sweet potatoes, scrubbed and chunked

1 tablespoon honey

¼ teaspoon ground ginger

2 teaspoons arrowroot starch

1 tablespoon cold water

Freshly ground pepper and herbal seasoning to taste

Place the meat and bay leaf in a large pot and cover with water or stock. Bring to a boil on top of the stove. Add the onions. Cook over medium heat for 40 minutes. Add the scrubbed and cut-up vegetables. Add the honey and ginger. Add more water or stock to cover—about an inch.

Simmer for 1 hour or until the meat is tender. Mix the arrowroot with a little cold water until smooth; then add a bit of the tsimmes broth and mix until smooth. Add this to the pot. Taste-check for seasoning. Cook gently for another 10 minutes.

Yield: 6 servings

and many more antioxidant carotenoids (as much as 15,750 international units in one cup of cooked carrots), as are sweet potatoes (15,600 units per cup).

Holiday Kreplach

DOUGH:

2 cups whole-wheat pastry flour

2 eggs, beaten

1 tablespoon water

½ teaspoon salt or herbal seasoning

Boiling water

Place the flour on a board and make a well in the center. In a bowl, combine the eggs, water, and seasoning. Pour the mixture into the well and work the flour into the liquid, kneading until smooth and elastic.

Roll out the dough on a floured surface. Cut the dough into 3-inch squares. Place a tablespoon of filling *(recipe below)* in the center of each. Fold the dough over, forming a triangle. Press the edges together neatly with a fork dipped in flour. Drop

Traditionally, kreplach are eaten three times during the year: on Purim, the seventh day of Sukkot, and the day before Yom Kippur. Kreplach are little squares of tender dough filled with meat, chicken, or cheese. This recipe calls for chicken or meat.

the kreplach, one by one, into boiling water. Cover tightly and cook for 20 minutes or until the kreplach rise to the top.

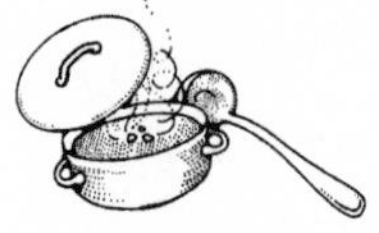

Yield: 24 or more, depending on how thin the dough has been rolled out

FILLING:

2 cups ground cooked chicken or meat

1 tablespoon minced onion

1 egg, beaten

1 tablespoon chopped fresh parsley

Combine all ingredients and the filling is ready to use.

Note: Kreplach may also be cooked in boiling soup. Or, after their water bath, they can be sprinkled with a little chicken fat or shpritzed with a little nonstick baking spray, then slipped into the oven for browning. Delicious every way.

VERENIKES

Verenikes are a rounded version of kreplach. They are usually filled with cheese, mashed potatoes, kasha, or cherries.

To make verenikes, follow the same recipe as for kreplach. For a real treat, fill them with pitted cherries, stewed and thickened with a little arrowroot or potato starch. Cook the verenikes in honey-sweetened cherry juice instead of water and serve hot in the juice. Delicious!

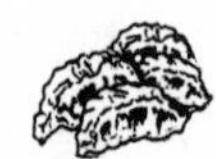

Honey-Apple Walnut Cake

This deliciously moist orange-flavored honey cake, made with cholesterol-lowering olive oil and oat bran, is appropriate at a Rosh Hashana afternoon tea, at a Yom Kippur break-the-fast meal, or spread with cream cheese for a lovely breakfast treat.

2 large eggs
½ cup orange juice concentrate, undiluted
⅓ cup olive oil
½ cup honey
1 teaspoon vanilla extract
1½ cups whole-wheat pastry flour
½ cup oat bran
1 teaspoon baking powder
½ teaspoon baking soda
¼ teaspoon grated nutmeg
2½ cups diced unpeeled apples
½ cup chopped walnuts

In a large mixing bowl or in a food processor using the steel blade, blend together the eggs, orange juice concentrate, oil, honey, and vanilla.

In a smaller bowl, combine the flour, oat bran, baking powder, baking soda, and nutmeg.

Combine the two mixtures and mix just to moisten the dry ingredients. Fold in the apples and nuts.

Line a 13 x 9 x 2–inch baking dish with parchment paper, or grease it lightly with a little oil, or use a vegetable-based cooking spray. Transfer the mixture to the baking dish.

Bake in a preheated 350-degree F. oven for 30 to 40 minutes or until a cake tester inserted in center of the cake comes out clean.

Cool on a rack. Cover and let stand overnight to allow time for the flavors to meld.

Yield: 8 to 10 servings

AMBROSIA CREAM

A delightfully refreshing and satisfying dish especially welcome after the long Yom Kippur fast.

1 can (20 ounces) **crushed pineapple**

2 oranges

1½ pints plain yogurt

½ cup coarsely chopped walnuts

½ cup unsweetened coconut flakes or shreds

1 pound seedless grapes plus any seasonal fruit

Drain the pineapple, reserving the juice for another use. Peel, section, and pit the oranges.

In a large glass bowl, combine the yogurt, pineapple, nuts, and coconut. Stir in the grapes and fruits, reserving a few orange sections for garnish.

Yield: 8 to 10 servings

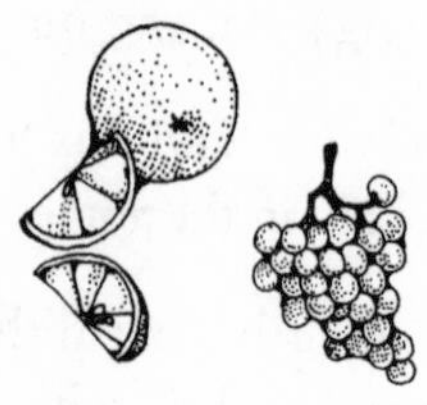

9

Enjoy a Happy, Healthy Chanukah

❧

O Chanukah, O Chanukah, a festival of joy,
A holiday, a jolly day for every girl and boy.
Spin the whirling dreidels all week long,
Eat the sizzling latkes, sing the happy songs.

Various versions of this little ditty will be sung in Jewish homes around the world as families gather together to sing "Rock of Ages" and light one new candle each night of Chanukah until the eight-candled menorah is aglow.

Then the story of the Maccabean struggle for the principle of religious freedom will be retold. Children will spin their dreidels with cries of "I win, you lose!" Presents will be exchanged, and then the sizzling latkes (pancakes) will be served.

Because of the oil used in their preparation, latkes are traditional for Chanukah, which literally means "dedication." We commemorate not so much the military victory as the cleansing and rededication of the Temple after it had been defiled.

Only a tiny bit of pure oil with which to rekindle the Eternal Light was found in the defiled Temple. The miracle of that little cruse of oil, which lasted for eight days, until more could be obtained, is considered symbolic of the miracle of the survival of the little Jewish nation, which through the ages has outlived powerful enemies.

While potato latkes and Chanukah are practically synonymous, cheese latkes and other dairy dishes are also traditional, for the enjoyment of dairy foods commemorates the bravery of the widow Judith. It is told that she entertained the Assyrian general Holofernes by feeding him great quantities of cheese and slaking his thirst with great quantities of wine, which made him incompetent to pursue the battle.

The question now is, can Chanukah be enjoyed without heartburn? In light of the new dietary guidelines, can we enjoy our culinary roots? How can we add Nutrition to Tradition?

These family-tested recipes will show you how you can be both traditional and contemporary. Enjoy these treats of Chanukah in the best of health.

Crispy Potato Latkes

5 medium-size unpeeled potatoes, well scrubbed and cubed

2 eggs

1 medium-size onion

¼ cup wheat germ, whole-wheat flour, or matzo meal

Freshly ground pepper and salt to taste, or omit the salt and use herbal seasoning or a dash of cinnamon

Oil for frying

In the bowl of a food processor, using the steel blade, blend together all ingredients. In a large frying pan, heat oil about ¼ inch deep until it sizzles. Drop the potato mixture by the tablespoonful into the hot oil. Brown well on both sides, then drain on several layers of paper toweling. Serve the latkes piping hot with applesauce, sour cream, or yogurt.

Yield: about 30 latkes, 6 to 8 servings

Baked Potato Latkes Variation: If you'd rather not fry the latkes, place them on an oiled cookie sheet and bake at 350 degrees F. for 45 minutes or until they are well browned. They're not quite so crispy as the fried, but they are good-tasting nonetheless.

Potato Kugel Variation: Pour the mixture into a greased 8 x 12–inch baking dish and place in a 350-degree F. oven for 45 minutes or until well browned. Cut into squares and serve piping hot.

Muffin Latkes Variation: Spoon the mixture into greased muffin tins and bake for about 30 minutes at 350 degrees F.

Note: You can freeze potato latkes, which will save

"They simmered, they shimmered, absorbing the olive oil. You may not guess, but it was the latkes that made the Syrians recoil." Use olive, peanut, or canola oil, all monounsaturates, which tend to reduce cholesterol levels and which, unlike the other classes of oil, remain stable when heated.

you lots of hassle when you have a big crowd of latke-lovers to feed. After making the latkes, place them on a cookie sheet, freeze, then transfer to a plastic bag for easy storage. When you are ready to serve, arrange them on a cookie sheet and heat in a 450-degree F. oven for about 5 minutes.

CHEESE LATKES

These would be great for breakfast, lunch, or as a side dish for a dairy dinner.

2 eggs, separated

1 cup cottage cheese

3 tablespoons oat bran or wheat germ

½ teaspoon honey

Beat the egg whites until stiff. Blend together the egg yolks and the remaining ingredients. Fold this mixture gently into the egg whites. Drop the batter by the tablespoonful onto a hot skillet that has been lightly greased or shpritzed with nonstick cooking spray. Sauté until lightly browned, then brown the flip side. Serve with yogurt, sour cream, applesauce, or berries.

Yield: about 26 latkes, 3 servings

Potato-Carrot Latkes

3 medium-size unpeeled carrots,
well scrubbed

3 medium-size unpeeled potatoes,
well scrubbed

1 medium-size onion

½ cup chopped fresh parsley

1 teaspoon lemon juice or ¼ teaspoon vitamin C powder

3 large eggs

¼ cup wheat germ or matzo meal

2 tablespoons oat bran

2 tablespoons lecithin granules

¼ teaspoon ground pepper, or to taste

Dash of ground cinnamon

½ teaspoon salt or kelp

Olive or peanut oil for frying

At least on one night of Chanukah, enjoy this variation on the traditional potato latke. You will be treating your family to a big helping of beta carotene and other carotenoids that have been shown to build resistance to cancer.

Cut the carrots, potatoes, and onion into chunks. In a food processor using the steel blade, blend all ingredients except the oil.

In a large heavy skillet, heat about ¼ inch of oil until it sizzles. Drop the batter by large spoonfuls into the hot oil to make each latke. Brown well on both sides, then drain on several layers of paper toweling. Serve piping hot with applesauce, sour cream, or yogurt.

Yield: about 36 crisp, delicious latkes; 6 to 8 servings

Muffin Variation: Pour the batter into greased muffin tins and bake in 350-degree F. oven for 20 to 30 minutes.

Kugel Variation: Pour the batter into a greased 9 x 9–

inch casserole and make a kugel.

Sesame Variation: For extra crispness, nutty flavor, and polyunsaturated nutrients, sprinkle latkes, muffins, or kugels with sesame seeds.

Applesauce for Latkes

Sweet—and no sugar.

1½ pounds unpeeled tart baking apples, washed

½ cup frozen apple juice concentrate, apple cider, or pineapple juice

½ teaspoon ground cinnamon, or to taste

Cut the apples in chunks and place in a large pot. Add the slightly thawed apple juice, cider, or pineapple juice. If you like a thinner sauce, add a little more liquid. Bring to a boil, then reduce the heat and let simmer for about 10 minutes. Let cool, then purée in the food processor or blender. This is the best applesauce that ever topped a latke!

Yield: 3 cups

Menorah Salads

You'll light up the faces around your table with these edible representations of the holiday. Children are very good at creating their own versions.

VEGETABLE MENORAH:

Stuff a long rib of celery with cream cheese or egg salad to make the base of the menorah.

Cut 8 carrot sticks of uniform size and place them in the stuffed celery stick. Top the carrot candles with bits of pimento, red pepper, or pomegranate seeds held in place with toothpicks.

FRUIT MENORAH:

Use a large peeled banana as the base of the menorah. Sprinkle with lemon juice. Use 8 carrot sticks for candles and pomegranate seeds or cherries for flames.

Candle Salads

Place a slice of pineapple, canned in its own juice, on a large lettuce leaf. Fit half of a peeled banana into the hole of the pineapple and attach a cherry or a pomegranate seed with a toothpick to the top of the banana.

To dress up the candlestick, give it a handle made of half an orange slice placed on the right side of the pineapple slice. Live it up and serve it with whipped cream!

Chanukah Symbol Cookies

1 egg
¼ cup thick applesauce
¼ cup olive or canola oil
¼ cup maple syrup
¼ cup unsulfured molasses
1 teaspoon vanilla extract
1½ tablespoons lemon or orange juice
1¾ cups whole-wheat pastry flour
2 tablespoons dry milk powder (or wheat germ for pareve)
2 tablespoons oat bran
1 teaspoon baking powder

To make these cookies pareve, substitute wheat germ for the dry milk powder. Symbol cookie cutters are usually available at your synagogue's gift shop. These delicious cookies provide half the fat of the usual cookie. Enjoy them!

In a mixing bowl or in the bowl of a food processor, blend together the egg, applesauce, oil, maple syrup, molasses, vanilla extract, and lemon or orange juice.

In another bowl, mix together the flour, milk powder or wheat germ, oat bran, and baking powder.

Combine the 2 mixtures and store the batter in the refrigerator until it reaches the soft-dough consistency. To do this, divide the dough in half, wrap each half in wax paper and refrigerate for several hours or overnight.

Roll out each portion of dough on a floured surface to about ⅛-inch thickness. With cookie cutters, cut into shapes representing the symbols of Chanukah. Place on cookie sheets, either lightly oiled or lined with parchment paper.

At this point, you can call in the troops and let them decorate the cookies with coconut, carob chips, sunflower seeds, chopped walnuts, and raisins.

Bake in a preheated 350-degree F. oven for 8 to 10 minutes. Watch them carefully lest they burn when you turn your back!

Yield: about 4 dozen cookies

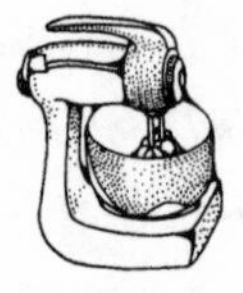

10

Putting Health in Your Purim Celebration

The holiday of Purim is a folk festival celebrated with the reading of Megillat Esther, feasting, merrymaking, masquerading, a lot of fun and foolishness, wine and hamantaschen.

On Purim, all the little girls dress up like Queen Esther, the heroine of the day, for it was she who saved the Jews from the gallows prepared for them by Haman, prime minister to King Ahasuerus. When Queen Esther revealed Haman's plot to the king, he ordered that Haman be hung on the gallows prepared for the Jewish people—and on the very date he had chosen for their destruction.

But, most of all Purim is a time for sharing.

One cannot be truly fulfilled without sharing one's joy and one's grief. Nothing has meaning unless it relates to others. That is why Purim is celebrated as a community event. Purim has meaning only when we celebrate together our being saved from Haman's evil decree.

The mitzvah of *mishloach manot,* the sending of gifts to others, is one expression of our link with our fellow Jews and of our concern for their welfare.

Gifts are traditionally hamantaschen or other baked goodies, fruits, nuts, and sometimes special surprises for the kinder.

The following recipes feature ingredients that are kind to your heart and will express your concern for others in the most meaningful way.

FRUIT-AND-NUT OAT-BRAN MUFFINS

Not only do these muffins contain no saturated fat to raise cholesterol levels and no concentrated sweetener to raise triglycerides, they are also rich in pectin, potassium, lecithin, and oat bran, all of which tend to lower cholesterol levels and enhance the health of the heart.

1 unpeeled apple, grated
1 cup raisins
1 cup chopped prunes
1 cup chopped walnuts
3 tablespoons oat bran
2 tablespoons lecithin granules
½ cup chopped almonds
3 egg whites, lightly beaten

In a mixing bowl, combine the apple, raisins, prunes, walnuts, oat bran, lecithin granules, and almonds. Add the egg whites and mix to moisten the ingredients.

Preheat the oven to 350 degrees F.

Line 3 dozen minimuffin cups with paper or foil liners, or spray with nonstick baking spray. Spoon the batter into the muffin cups and bake for 15 minutes.

Yield: 3 dozen minimuffins

Heart-to-Heart Chewy Nuggets

¼ cup olive oil
¼ cup honey or molasses
1 egg
1 teaspoon vanilla extract
⅓ cup whole-wheat pastry flour
2 tablespoons lecithin granules
2 tablespoons oat bran
½ teaspoon ground cinnamon
1 tablespoon grated orange rind
¼ cup sunflower seeds
½ cup rolled oats
½ cup chopped nuts

Preheat the oven to 350 degrees F.

In a food processor, blender, or mixing bowl, combine the oil, honey or molasses, egg, and vanilla. Process or mix until smooth and creamy.

In another bowl, combine the flour, lecithin, oat bran, cinnamon, orange rind, sunflower seeds, and rolled oats. Blend this mixture with the oil mixture until the ingredients are well combined.

Spoon the batter into a 9-inch-square baking pan lined with parchment paper or coated with nonstick baking spray. Sprinkle the nuts over the batter. Bake for 20 to 25 minutes or until a cake tester inserted in the center comes out clean. Cool slightly, then cut into 1½-inch squares.

Yield: 36 nuggets

These nutty, chewy treats will delight your palate and gladden your heart. They are enriched with olive oil, a monounsaturate which has been shown to be a winner in the cholesterol wars—even better than the polyunsaturates, which tend to lower both the bad and the good cholesterol levels. The monounsaturates, on the other hand, lower the LDL, which is associated with increased risk of cardiovascular problems; but they don't affect the HDL, which has been found to protect against heart problems.

HAMANTASCHEN

The whole wheat flour, oat bran, and lecithin granules in the crust bring a measure of preventive medicine to your enjoyment of this happy holiday. The prunes and apricots in the fillings are goldmines of vitamin A. Poppy seeds (mohn) are a good source of the B vitamins and many minerals, including zinc, which, like vitamin A, is an important antioxidant.

DOUGH:

2 eggs

3 tablespoons canola oil

¼ cup honey

1¾ cups whole-wheat pastry flour

1½ teaspoons baking powder

¼ cup oat bran

2 tablespoons lecithin granules

1 teaspoon grated lemon or orange rind

In a food processor, using the steel blade, blend the eggs, oil, and honey.

In another bowl, combine the flour, baking powder, oat bran, lecithin granules, and lemon or orange rind.

Add the dry ingredients to the food processor and whiz until the ingredients form a ball.

On a floured surface, roll out the dough about ⅛-inch thick. Cut into 3½-inch rounds. Place a heaping teaspoon of filling *(see below)* in the center of each round. Draw up two "sides" of the dough, then the third "side." Pinch the edges together to form a three-cornered pocket.

Bake the hamantaschen on a cookie sheet shpritzed with nonstick baking spray, or lined with parchment paper, in a 375-degree F. oven for 30 minutes or until nicely browned.

Yield: 24 small or 12 large hamantaschen

PRUNE FILLING:

1 pound sweet pitted prunes

4 thin orange slices, including the peel

Rind and juice of ½ lemon

½ cup chopped walnuts or sunflower seeds

2 tablespoons honey

Dash of ground cinnamon

Toss the prunes with the orange slices and let stand for several hours or overnight. (Or, mix the prunes with a few tablespoons of orange juice or water, then cover and microcook on high for about 3 minutes.) Add the lemon rind and juice and purée in a food processor or blender. Add the remaining ingredients.

Yield: enough filling for 12 large or 24 small hamantaschen

VARIATIONS:

1. Use half prunes and half dried apricots.
2. Use all apricots.
3. Use apricots, raisins, and prunes.
4. Add ½ cup almonds to the dried fruit and purée.
5. Substitute ½ cup granola for the nuts.

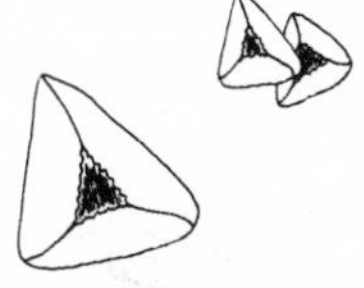

POPPY SEED (MOHN) FILLING:

2 cups poppy seeds
Boiling water
¼ cup honey
1 cup water
¼ teaspoon ground cinnamon
Pinch of powdered ginger
1 egg, well beaten
1 tablespoon grated orange peel
½ cup raisins

Put the seeds in a large bowl. Pour boiling water over them. When the seeds settle to the bottom of the bowl, drain off the water. Grind the seeds fine.

In a large saucepan, combine the ground poppy seeds, honey, water, cinnamon, and ginger. Cook over low heat until thick—about 1 hour—stirring frequently. Let the mixture cool, then add the beaten egg, the orange peel, and the raisins.

Yield: enough filling for 12 large or 24 small hamantaschen

VARIATIONS:

1. Add ½ cup finely chopped walnuts, almonds, or sunflower seeds or ¼ cup fine granola crumbs to the filling.
2. Instead of the orange peel, use 2 teaspoons frozen orange juice concentrate, thawed but undiluted.

Tahina-Oatmeal-Walnut Cookies

Tahina, made from sesame seeds, is an excellent source of essential fatty acids, so important to maintaining smooth beautiful skin and to preventing damaging deposits of cholesterol.

6 tablespoons tahina (sesame butter)
½ cup honey
½ cup chopped walnuts
1 cup rolled oats
½ teaspoon ground cinnamon

Preheat the oven to 325 degrees F.

In a medium-size mixing bowl, stir together the tahina and honey. Add the nuts, then the oats and cinnamon. Mix to blend the ingredients.

Onto a cookie sheet lined with parchment paper greased with a few drops of oil or sprayed with nonstick cooking spray, drop the batter a teaspoonful at a time. Bake for 10 to 12 minutes.

Yield: 30 to 36 cookies

Triple-Decker Prune and Apricot Fluden

A delicious blend of tart, sweet, smooth, and crunchy, these bars are simple to prepare and can be cut into triangles to simulate Haman's hat.

BOTTOM LAYER:

1 cup whole-wheat pastry flour
½ teaspoon ground cinnamon
2 tablespoons softened butter or oil
2 tablespoons honey
¼ cup applesauce

MIDDLE LAYER:

10 prunes, pitted and chopped

10 dried apricots, chopped

1 cup orange juice

1 teaspoon grated orange rind

2 teaspoons arrowroot starch or cornstarch

1 cup chopped nuts

TOP LAYER:

2 eggs

1 teaspoon vanilla extract

½ cup grated unsweetened coconut

½ cup chopped walnuts

To make the bottom layer, combine the flour and cinnamon. Set aside. In a small mixing bowl, cream the butter or oil with the honey and applesauce. Beat in the flour and cinnamon. Pat the mixture into the bottom of ungreased 9 x 9–inch baking dish and bake at 350 degrees F. for 10 minutes or until just tinged with gold. Let cool for about 15 minutes before adding the middle layer.

To make the middle layer, place the prunes, apricots, and orange juice in a saucepan and cook over medium heat for 10 minutes. Add the grated orange rind and the starch. Bring to a boil, reduce the heat, and simmer, stirring constantly for a few minutes or until the mixture thickens. Stir in the nuts. Spread over the cooled bottom later.

To make the top layer, beat the eggs in a small bowl until frothy. Stir in the vanilla, coconut, and walnuts. Spread evenly over the cooled fruit mixture and bake for 25 to 30 minutes at 350 degrees F. Cool, then cut into 1½-inch squares or triangles.

Yield: 36 pieces

11

CHICKEN— NOT JUST FOR SHABBAT

It just wouldn't be Shabbat dinner without chicken. But chicken is not just for Shabbat anymore. And that is healthy progress. Chicken and its cousins in the poultry family are less costly, less fatty, and higher in nutritional value in proportion to calories than either beef or lamb.

As little as 3½ ounces of chicken or turkey provides an impressive 28 to 31 grams of protein. (The light meat has a higher protein value and less fat than the dark, though the differences are slight.) It also provides potassium, iron, phosphorus, and some calcium.

Chicken also provides some vitamin A, which has antioxidant value, and both chicken and turkey provide B vitamins with a real high in cholesterol-lowering niacin. Gone are the days when we bought chickens live and took them to the *shochet* (ritual slaughterer). Gone are the little *eyerlach* (eggs without shells) which we found inside the chickens; they were cooked with great care and doled out to the children with love and chicken soup. And very rarely can you find a chicken with feet, which add gelatin and body to the soup.

But, I am happy to report, there is now a source through which you can obtain not only chicken *feeselach* but also natural, free-range, ready-to-cook kosher chickens and turkeys that have been fed grain grown without herbicides, pesticides, antibiotics, preservatives, or any artificial ingredients. They can be ordered from Wise Kosher Natural Poultry, 197 Williamsburg Street West, Brooklyn, New York 11211.

Many cooks remove the skin of the fowl, then add fat of some kind for moisture. I prefer to use the fat that is indigenous to the source. I leave the skin on. The fat in the chicken skin not only makes for a deliciously moist and flavorful chicken dish, but also one that is kinder to your heart. The fat in chicken skin is mainly monounsaturated, the kind that tends to lower harmful cholesterol levels. It is not necessary to eat the skin if you're counting calories. Just cook with it and limit the addition of other fats.

For good health and that lovely Shabbat taste, enjoy the following recipes.

How to Prepare Schmaltz and Grieben

Various recipes throughout the book call for schmaltz—rendered chicken fat—or grieben, the crisp pieces that remain after the fat and skin have been rendered. Preparation is fast and easy and worth every bit of effort. Here's how:

Cut the fatty skin and globules of fat into small pieces. Place in a heavy pot and cook over low heat until the fat is almost liquid. Add a coarsely chopped onion and continue cooking until the onion is tinged with gold and the skins are temptingly brown and crisp. Watch carefully. They tend to burn when you turn your back on them. Let the pot cool a little, then strain into a clean jar to separate the schmaltz from the grieben.

MICROWAVE METHOD:

Put the skin and fat in a microsafe bowl and cook on high for 2 minutes. Add the coarsely chopped onion and cook on medium for another 2 minutes. Pour off the schmaltz into a clean jar and remove the onions if they are crisp and golden. If the skins are not yet crisp, cook in one minute increments until they are brown and crisp.

Both the schmaltz and the grieben may be stored in the refrigerator, or, for longer periods of time, in the freezer.

Chicken Soup with Flanken

3 quarts water or vegetable stock

1 piece of flanken (about 1½ pounds)

Several marrow bones

1 pullet (about 4 pounds), cut into quarters

Giblets except the liver

3 small onions

2 carrots, quartered

2 stalks celery with leaves

1 parsley root (optional)

1 bay leaf

1 tablespoon chopped fresh dill or ½ teaspoon dill seed

Several sprigs of parsley

¼ teaspoon ground ginger

Freshly ground pepper, salt, or vegetable seasoning, to taste

In a large pot, bring the water or stock to a boil. Add the flanken and bones. Simmer for 30 minutes, then skim.

Add the chicken, giblets, vegetables, and the seasonings. Simmer for 1 hour or until the chicken and meat are tender. Serve with brown rice, noodles, or knaidlach.

Yield: 4 to 6 servings

Note: If your family doesn't particularly relish boiled chicken, remove the chicken after 45 minutes of cooking in the soup. Put it in a baking dish, rub with garlic, sprinkle with lemon juice, paprika, ginger, thyme, dry mustard, and a little sage. Roast in a preheated 350-degree F. oven, uncovered, until deliciously brown.

What is it about hot chicken soup that gives it the ability to cure a cold? Nobody knows. Is it the aroma? Whatever it is, doctors say, there's "something extra" in chicken soup. Could it be the Sabbath taste?

Roast Chicken with Lemon and Wine

This is my family's favorite. It's simple, quick, moist, tender, and flavorful.

1 whole chicken (about 3½ pounds)

Juice of 1 lemon

1 garlic clove, crushed

½ teaspoon ground ginger

½ teaspoon dry mustard

¼ teaspoon crushed dried sage

1 teaspoon paprika

½ cup dry white wine

Preheat the oven to 350 degrees F.

Clean the chicken and remove all visible fat. Sprinkle with the lemon juice and rub with the crushed garlic and dry seasonings inside and out.

Place the chicken in the roasting pan. Add the wine. Bake for 1¼ hours or until the juices run clear without a hint of pink.

Yield: 4 servings

Polynesian Chicken with Pineapple

If you can't go to Hawaii, you can enjoy its spirit and flavor with this quick and easy dish.

1 can (20 ounces) **unsweetened pineapple chunks with juice**

1 tablespoon reduced-sodium soy sauce

2 tablespoons lemon juice

1 tablespoon honey

½ teaspoon minced fresh ginger

1 tablespoon minced onion

1 broiler chicken (about 3 pounds), cut into eighths

In a large bowl, combine all the ingredients except the chicken. Place the chicken parts in another large bowl and pour the pineapple marinade over it. Refrigerate for 1 hour.

Preheat the oven to 350 degrees F.

Place the chicken parts with the marinade in a roasting pan and place in the preheated oven. Cover and bake for about 1 hour. Remove the cover for the last 15 minutes of baking.

Yield: 6 servings

AUNT BETTY'S CHICKEN CACCIATORE EMBRACED WITH LIFESAVING VEGETABLES

The carrots, zucchini, sweet potatoes, onions, garlic, and tomatoes provide a plethora of protective antioxidants, making this dish not only a prescription for good health but a joy to eat.

2 large unpeeled carrots, scrubbed or scraped and sliced diagonally

1 large unpeeled zucchini, scrubbed and cut into 2-inch chunks

2 medium-size unpeeled potatoes, scrubbed and cut into quarters

2 medium-size unpeeled sweet potatoes, scrubbed and cut into 2-inch chunks

2 medium-size onions, cut into chunks

1 can (28 ounces) **tomatoes**

2 teaspoons crushed dried basil

1 teaspoon crushed dried oregano

¼ cup chopped fresh parsley or 2 teaspoons dried

1 teaspoon minced garlic

¼ teaspoon freshly ground pepper

1 broiler-fryer chicken (about 3 pounds), cut into serving-size pieces

Preheat the oven to 350 degrees F.

In a large roasting pan, arrange all the vegetables. Add the tomatoes with juice. Sprinkle with the herbs and spices. Place the chicken pieces on top.

Bake for 1½ hours or until the chicken and vegetables are tender.

Yield: 6 servings

Chicken Seville

1 tablespoon canola oil or schmaltz

1 broiler-fryer chicken (about 3 pounds), cut into serving pieces, **or 2 chicken breasts** with all visible fat removed

1 large green or red bell pepper, chopped

1 medium-size tomato, chopped

¼ teaspoon freshly ground pepper, or to taste

2 navel oranges, peeled and separated into segments

In a Dutch oven or large heavy skillet with a tight-fitting lid, heat the oil or schmaltz.

When the fat begins to bubble, add the chicken skin-side down. Cook over medium-high heat for 10 minutes or until the skin is golden brown. Turn over the chicken pieces and cook for 5 more minutes.

Add the chopped bell pepper, tomato, and ground pepper. Add the orange sections. Cover tightly and cook over low heat for about 40 minutes.

Yield: 4 to 6 servings

Oranges contribute vitamin C, potassium, and a delightful flavor to this refreshingly different Spanish specialty.

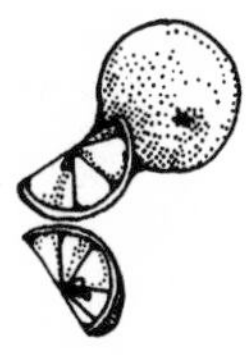

Mexican Baked Chicken Flavored with Carob and Cinnamon

Enjoy South-of-the-Border flavors without leaving home. A deliciously spicy dish. Serve with a cool cucumber salad.

1 broiler-fryer chicken (about 3 pounds), cut into serving-size pieces and all visible fat removed

1 teaspoon herbal seasoning

¼ teaspoon freshly ground pepper

1 red or green bell pepper, seeds removed and cut into strips

1 can (8 ounces) **tomato sauce**

2 tablespoons fruit juice–sweetened apricot conserves or orange marmalade

1 tablespoon carob powder or unsweetened cocoa

½ teaspoon Tabasco sauce

½ teaspoon ground cinnamon

2 teaspoons sesame seeds

Place the chicken pieces in a baking dish and sprinkle with the herbal seasoning and pepper. Place the bell pepper strips over the chicken.

In a bowl, combine the tomato sauce, apricot conserves or orange marmalade, carob or cocoa, Tabasco sauce, and cinnamon. Drizzle this mixture over the chicken. Sprinkle with sesame seeds. Cover with foil or parchment paper and bake at 375 degrees F. for 45 minutes. Remove the foil or parchment paper and bake 15 minutes longer.

Yield: 6 servings

Chicken and Banana Barbecue

A delightful marriage of flavors and textures.

1 broiler-fryer chicken (about 3 pounds), quartered

½ cup ketchup

2 tablespoons vinegar (wine or apple cider)

1 tablespoon prepared mustard

2 tablespoons minced onion

3 medium-ripe bananas, peeled and cut into chunks

Wash the chicken and trim away all visible fat. Place the chicken, skin side up, in a casserole or baking dish.

In a small bowl, mix together the ketchup, vinegar, mustard, and onion.

Spoon about three-quarters of the sauce over the chicken and bake in a 375-degree F. oven for 40 minutes. Add the bananas to the chicken. Brush the bananas with the remaining sauce and return the dish to the oven for another 10 minutes. Serve piping hot.

Yield: 4 servings

CHICKEN CHOP SUEY

This dish contains fresh bean sprouts, an excellent source of antioxidants. For vegetarians, substitute tofu for the chicken.

½ cup chopped onion

1 cup chopped celery

½ cup chopped green or red bell pepper

1 cup sliced mushrooms

2 teaspoons oil or chicken fat

2 cups cut-up cooked chicken, or 1 cup chicken and 1 cup tofu (all tofu for vegetarians)

2 cups chicken stock (vegetable stock for vegetarians)

1 tablespoon low-sodium Tamari soy sauce

2 tablespoons arrowroot starch or cornstarch

¼ cup cold water

1 cup fresh mung bean sprouts

In a heavy-bottomed skillet or wok, sauté the onion, celery, green or red pepper, and mushrooms in the oil or chicken fat until just tender.

Add the chicken or tofu, chicken or vegetable stock, and soy sauce. Simmer, stirring constantly, for about 10 minutes or until the ingredients are heated through.

Dissolve the starch in the cold water and add gradually, stirring until the chop suey is thickened.

Just before serving, add the bean sprouts.

Yield: 6 to 8 servings

Cashew Chicken or Turkey à la King

A delicious and nutritious party dish that the family will love.

½ cup unsalted cashew nuts

2 tablespoons chicken or vegetable stock

1 onion, diced

1 cup sliced fresh mushrooms or ½ cup canned

1 green or red bell pepper, seeded and diced

2 cups chicken soup or vegetable stock

¼ teaspoon curry powder

1 tablespoon arrowroot starch or cornstarch

2 tablespoons cold water

2 cups cut-up cooked chicken or turkey

Roast the cashews lightly in a 250-degree F. oven for about 8 minutes, or in the microwave on high for about 2 minutes. Set aside.

In a large deep skillet, heat the 2 tablespoons of stock. Sauté the onion, mushrooms, and pepper in the stock for about 3 minutes, until softened. Add the 2 cups of soup or stock and the curry powder.

In a small bowl, thoroughly combine the starch and water. Add to the skillet and bring to a boil. Add the cut-up chicken or turkey. Sprinkle on the roasted cashews.

Serve over hot brown rice, whole-grain toast, in patty shells, or as a stuffing for baked potatoes.

Yield: 4 to 6 servings

CHICKEN PAPRIKASH WITH NOODLES

The piquant sauce of this Hungarian-style dish permeates the chicken and the noodles, creating a full-bodied dish with Old World Nostalgia.

2 broiler-fryer chickens (2 to 3 pounds each), cut into serving-size pieces

1 cup chopped onion

1 tablespoon paprika

1 tablespoon whole-wheat flour

1 teaspoon herbal seasoning

¼ teaspoon ground pepper

1 can (8 ounces) **whole tomatoes**

1 pound broad egg noodles, cooked following package directions

Remove all visible fat and some of the skin from the chickens. Place in a large heavy skillet, and render the chicken fat and skin.

Brown the chicken pieces in the rendered fat. Remove the browned chicken from the skillet and sauté the onion in the pan drippings until soft.

Stir in the paprika and flour. Cook, stirring constantly, for 1 minute. Stir in the herbal seasoning, pepper, and tomatoes. Break up the tomatoes with a wooden spoon.

Add the chicken. Turn to coat each piece. Cover the skillet and simmer for 20 minutes. Turn the chicken pieces. Simmer 15 minutes longer, or until the chicken is tender.

Place the hot noodles on a serving platter. Arrange the chicken on the noodles. Bring the sauce in the skillet to a boil. Spoon the hot sauce over the noodles and chicken just before serving.

Yield: 8 servings

Yonah's Chicken n' Coke

A weird combination, I agree. But, my Israeli friend Yonah told me it won top honors in a chicken recipe contest. Chicken with Coca Cola sounded bizarre, so naturally I wanted to try it. But I had no Coke, so I substituted pineapple juice. For the ketchup, I substituted tomato sauce. I was amazed at how good it was. Then I tried the original Coca Cola version. It was also surprisingly good. Try it. Then, for improved nutritional value, try my revised version (with the pineapple juice and tomato sauce).

2 medium-size onions, chopped

½ cup Coca Cola Classic (or ½ cup unsweetened pineapple juice)

½ cup ketchup (or tomato sauce)

2 tablespoons vinegar, preferably balsamic

½ cup fruit juice–sweetened apricot conserves

2 tablespoons Worcestershire sauce

½ teaspoon chili powder

3 medium-size sweet potatoes, peeled and cut into ½-inch chunks

2 small chickens (about 2½ pounds each), cut into serving-size pieces

In a heavy saucepan, combine all ingredients except the sweet potatoes and chickens. Bring to a boil, reduce the heat, and simmer, covered, for about 30 minutes, until the sauce is thickened, stirring occasionally.

Arrange the chicken pieces in an ovenproof casserole. Arrange the sweet potatoes around the chicken. Pour the prepared sauce over all. Bake at 350 degrees F. for 1 hour or until chicken is tender.

Yield: 8 servings

CHICKEN WITH ROZHINKES AND MANDLEN (RAISINS AND ALMONDS)

An exotic melange of flavors and textures.

½ tablespoon chicken fat, canola oil, or olive oil

½ onion, chopped

1 large garlic clove, minced

1 teaspoon carob powder

½ teaspoon chili powder

¼ teaspoon ground cumin

1 can (8 ounces) **tomato sauce,** preferably salt-free

¼ cup raisins

¼ cup slivered or chopped almonds, or sunflower seeds

2 tablespoons fruit juice-sweetened apricot conserves

¼ cup water or apple juice

1 tablespoon wheat germ

4 chicken thighs, trimmed of all visible fat

Preheat the oven to 400 degrees F.

In a 12-inch skillet, preferably nonstick, heat the chicken fat or oil. Add the onion and garlic and sauté for about 1 minute. Stir in the carob powder, chili powder, and cumin and cook for another minute.

Stir in the tomato sauce, raisins, almonds or sunflower seeds, apricot conserves, water or apple juice, and wheat germ. Reduce the heat and simmer for about 10 minutes. Place the chicken in a heatproof casserole and bake for 15 minutes.

Drizzle a quarter-cup of the sauce over each piece

of chicken and bake for another 15 minutes or until the chicken is tender and the juices run clear. Serve with baked potatoes or cooked brown rice.

Yield: 4 servings

ORANGE CHICKEN STIR-FRY

Sweet red peppers and flavorful grapes enhance the succulence and antioxidant value of this very tasty dish.

4 tablespoons orange juice, divided

1½ pounds boneless chicken breasts, cut into 1-inch pieces

1 medium-size red bell pepper, seeded and cut into small chunks

3 teaspoons grated orange zest

1 teaspoon grated fresh ginger root or ½ teaspoon ground ginger

2 garlic cloves, minced

½ cup chopped onion or 2 scallions, thinly sliced

½ teaspoon Tabasco or other hot pepper sauce

1 tablespoon arrowroot starch or cornstarch

1 cup orange juice

1 orange, sectioned

1 cup seedless red or white grapes, halved

1 tablespoon reduced-sodium soy sauce

In a wok or large nonstick skillet, heat 2 tablespoons of the orange juice. Add the cut-up chicken and stir-fry for 2 minutes. Add the cut-up red pepper, orange zest, ginger root or powder, garlic, onion or scallions, and hot pepper sauce to the wok or skillet and stir-fry for 5 minutes.

In a cup, blend the starch with the remaining 2 tablespoons of the orange juice, then combine with the 1 cup of juice and add to the stir-fry. Add the orange sections, grapes, and soy sauce to the pan, and heat on medium-high until the sauce thickens. Serve with hot brown rice.

Yield: 6 servings

12

ENJOY KUGELS, KNISHES, AND BLINTZES (That Are High in Fiber and Low in Fat)

Kugels

Kugels (puddings) are a wonderful convenience food. They can be made ahead and stored in the freezer in anticipation of a Bar Mitzvah, a *brit,* a dinner party, or an invasion of college kids home for semester break. The wave of joyful gustatory nostalgia that kugels evoke warms your heart and theirs.

But, let's face it. Kugels can be nutritional disasters. Most recipes call for enough sugar and fat to give you a toothache, clogged arteries, and an expanded waistline. If you want to do a real good deed, serve kugels that are kind to the cardiovascular system and a pleasure to the palate.

HOW? LET ME SHOW YOU.

Kugels come in infinite variety—potato, barley, rice, noodle—just about any starchy substance combined with eggs and appropriate spices and you have the ingredients for a kugel. *Lukshen* (noodle) kugels are the most popular. Most noodles are made from white flour. Whole-wheat noodles are available at health food stores. But, to get started on this healthy adventure without turning your family off, I suggest you use the noodles they are accustomed to and enrich the kugel yourself.

The philosophy behind *cooking kosher the new way* is simply to add to each ingredient the nutrients that would have been there in the first place if that food had not been emasculated in the refining process.

Since both wheat germ and bran have been removed from white flour, unbleached as well as bleached, use these health-building ingredients whenever you use a white-flour product. Wheat germ provides vitamin E and potassium so necessary to heart health and stroke protection. Bran is an important source of fiber.

Dairy lukshen kugels call for a lot of fat, which can be a troublemaker when it gangs up in your arteries and forms clots. In order to help prevent this eventuality, I use lecithin granules, a substance which emulsifies fat and, according to a recent research study done in Israel, significantly lowers both cholesterol and triglyceride levels.

Please don't load your kugels with sugar even if your favorite recipe calls for it. If your family is accustomed to sweet kugels, reduce the amount of sweetener gradually. Switch to honey instead of sugar and use half the amount the recipe calls for. Gradually reduce the amount of honey as well. Soon, the usual kugels served at Bar Mitzvahs will taste much too sweet to your family and you will be able to say *mazel tov,* their tastebuds have been educated.

Dairy Kugel

A delicious kugel you can enjoy with a fish or vegetarian meal, or serve it for a special breakfast or brunch.

8 ounces fine noodles
⅛ pound (4 tablespoons) **butter**
2 tablespoons honey
¼ cup sour cream
¼ cup plain yogurt
8 ounces cottage cheese
2 tablespoons wheat germ
2 tablespoons wheat or oat bran
2 tablespoons lecithin granules
1 cup milk
3 eggs, well beaten
Dash of cinnamon
Sesame seeds for garnish

Boil the noodles in lightly salted water and drain.

Melt the butter in an 8 x 10–inch baking dish. Add the melted butter to the noodles, leaving a little in the baking dish. Add the rest of the ingredients, except the sesame seeds, to the noodles. Transfer the noodle mixture to the baking dish. Top with the sesame seeds.

Bake in a preheated 350-degree F. oven for 1 hour or until nicely browned. Delicious served with yogurt and crushed strawberries.

Yield: 8 to 10 servings

CRUNCHY FLEISHIG KUGEL

Fantastic with chicken. Light as a soufflé, with a crunchy crust and a Shabbasdik flavor.

8 ounces fine noodles, boiled and drained (reserve 4 tablespoons of liquid)

6 eggs, well beaten

2 tablespoons bran soaked in 4 tablespoons of the water drained from the cooked noodles

½ cup wheat germ

2 tablespoons lecithin granules

Dash of ground cinnamon

Ground white pepper to taste

4 tablespoons olive oil or chicken fat

Sesame seeds

In a large mixing bowl, combine the noodles, eggs, the soaked bran, wheat germ, lecithin granules, cinnamon, and pepper.

Heat 2 tablespoons of the oil or chicken fat in an 8 x 10-baking dish. Pour the noodle mixture into the baking dish and top with lots of sesame seeds. Drizzle the remaining oil or chicken fat on top.

Bake in a preheated 400-degree F. oven for 15 minutes, then lower the temperature to 350 degrees F. and bake for another 35 minutes or until brown and crusty.

Yield: 8 to 10 servings

Potato Kugel

1 medium-size onion, diced

3 large unpeeled potatoes, scrubbed and diced

2 tablespoons wheat germ

2 tablespoons oat bran

2 tablespoons wheat bran

2 tablespoons lecithin granules

3 eggs

⅛ **teaspoon white pepper,** or to taste

1 teaspoon kosher salt or herbal seasoning

2 tablespoons olive oil or chicken fat

Preheat the oven to 350 degrees F.

In a food processor, combine the onion and potatoes. Process until coarsely puréed. Add the remaining ingredients except the oil or chicken fat and process to combine the ingredients.

Heat 1 tablespoon of fat in a 9 x 9–inch baking dish. Add the potato mixture. Top with the remaining fat. Bake for about 1 hour, until the kugel is brown and crisp. Serve with applesauce.

Yield: 6 to 8 servings

Potatoes are a good energy food, an excellent source of fiber, and are low in calories. There are only 90 calories in a 5-ounce potato, which also provides 20 milligrams of vitamin C, as much protein as provided by a half-glass of milk, iron, and niacin, the B vitamin that has been shown to lower cholesterol levels. A real nutritional bargain!

Pineapple Whole-Wheat Lukshen Kugel

The whole-wheat noodles in this kugel cook up almost white and have a robust, satisfying flavor. The kugel can also be made with white noodles. If so, add 3 tablespoons of wheat germ to the ingredients.

8 ounces medium whole-wheat noodles
1 pound cottage cheese
1 cup lite sour cream or plain yogurt
2 tablespoons lecithin granules
1 cup milk
1 can (20 ounces) **crushed pineapple,** drained
3 eggs, beaten
2 tablespoons honey
2 tablespoons unsalted butter, melted
½ cup raisins
1 teaspoon vanilla extract
Ground cinnamon

Cook the noodles according to package directions and drain. Preheat the oven to 350 degrees F.

In a large bowl, combine all ingredients including the noodles. Pour into an 11 x 14–inch baking dish greased with nonstick spray or butter. Bake for 1 hour or until the top is crusty and golden.

Yield: 8 to 10 servings

CUSTARDY APPLE KUGEL

A delicious kugel that can be enjoyed in good health. The yogurt and the pectin in the apple tend to lower harmful cholesterol. Pectin also helps rid the body of lead and actually puts the brakes on runaway appetites, making it easier to stay slim.

8 ounces medium noodles

⅔ cup lowfat milk plus 2 teaspoons dry milk powder

1 cup plain yogurt

8 ounces lowfat cottage cheese

1 large unpeeled apple (there's a lot of pectin in the peel), grated

2 tablespoons honey or pure maple syrup

¼ cup wheat germ

½ teaspoon vanilla extract

Juice of ½ lemon

½ cup raisins

4 eggs

2 tablespoons unsalted butter

1 scant teaspoon ground cinnamon, or as you like it

3 tablespoons chopped walnuts

Cook the noodles according to package directions and drain. (Try artichoke noodles if you can find them. They're low in calories and high in nutrients.)

In a bowl, combine the milk, milk powder, and yogurt. Add the cottage cheese and mix well. Add the grated apple, honey or syrup, wheat germ, vanilla, lemon juice, and raisins. Fold into the noodles.

Preheat the oven to 325 degrees F. Beat the eggs well and reserve.

Heat an 8 x 10–inch baking dish in the oven for 10 minutes. Melt the butter in the heated dish. Pour in the cheese-noodle mixture. Pour the beaten eggs on top. Sprinkle with cinnamon and the chopped walnuts. Bake for an hour or until nicely browned.

Yield: 8 to 10 servings

CARROT KUGEL

This pareve kugel—a goldmine of beta carotene and other carotenoids—is great hot or cold. Serve with chicken and a salad for a meal rich in life-saving antioxidants.

2 large carrots, grated

2 tablespoons canola or peanut oil

2 eggs, separated

¼ cup honey

1 cup whole-wheat pastry flour

½ teaspoon baking powder

1 teaspoon vanilla extract

3 teaspoon grated lemon rind

½ cup raisins

½ cup sunflower seeds or chopped walnuts

In a bowl, combine the carrots, oil, egg yolks, and honey. Add the flour, baking powder, vanilla, grated rind, raisins, and seeds or nuts.

Beat the egg whites until stiff and fold in. Transfer the mixture to a loaf pan shpritzed with nonstick spray or coated with a little oil. Bake in a preheated 350-degree F. oven for 35 minutes or until nicely browned.

Yield: 6 servings

Knishes Can be a Healthy Pleasure

In Israel, street vendors sell knishes on Purim, when crowds are singing, dancing, and eating in the streets. There's something about the crispy crust and the savory filling that enhances the merrymaking.

In America, knishes are frequently served at cocktail parties and on festive occasions. Usually they are made from white flour, which lacks the lifegiving nutrients and antioxidants of the wheat germ that was removed in the refining process. In addition, they are usually highly salted and too fatty for good health.

To make a meal very special, make knishes from whole wheat and soy flours. (Soy products contain a substance found to retard the development of malignancies.) Reduce the fat and make them tasty without a lot of salt, as suggested in the following recipe.

Fill them with cheese, potato, liver, kasha, or rice. You'll find that even noneaters, the ones who hang around the table just for the conversation, will consume these "healthy pleasures" with gusto.

Knish Crust

This crust is more than a blanket for a savory filling. The combination of wheat and soy make it a wholesome complete protein in its own right.

1½ cups sifted whole-wheat pastry flour

2 tablespoons soy flour

½ teaspoon salt or 1 teaspoon no-salt vegetable seasoning

1 egg

2 tablespoons unsalted butter or monounsaturated oil (canola, olive, or peanut)

6 tablespoons warm water

In a large bowl, combine the flours and salt or seasoning. In a separate bowl, beat the egg with the fat (butter for dairy fillings, oil for pareve or meat fillings) and water.

Pour the liquid mixture over the dry ingredients. Mix well. Knead lightly until the dough is no longer sticky. Form the dough into a ball and place it in a greased (use oil or nonstick spray) bowl slightly larger than the ball of dough. Cover and set in a warm place for an hour.

Cover your kitchen table with an old tablecloth. Rub some flour into it. Divide the dough in half. Roll out each piece as thin as possible into a large rectangle. Stretch and pull carefully until the dough is as thin as tissue paper and you can see the pattern of the tablecloth through it. If it should tear, patch it with a piece from the edge and roll it in.

Place filling (see recipes below) in a thick line across the edge of the rolled-out dough about 4 inches from the edge nearest you. Bend this edge over the filling. Now, gently raise the tablecloth and let it roll away from you.

Preheat the oven to 375 degrees F. With the little-finger edge of your hand, segment the roll into 1-inch sections. Use a knife to complete the cutting. Pull the dough at the ends of each section over the exposed filling and pat it between your hands. At this point, my Mom would say, “Be a knish.”

Shpritz a cookie sheet with nonstick spray. Place the knishes carefully—about ½ inch apart—on the prepared cookie sheet. Bake for 45 minutes or until crisp, light brown, and redolent with appetite-teasing aromas.

Yield: about 12 knishes, 6 servings

Note: If you plan to freeze the knishes for later use, bake for 30 minutes, allow to cool, then freeze.

Tasty Fillings for Knishes

The recipes below will yield enough filling for the Knish Crust recipe above.

POTATO FILLING (FLEISHIG):

2 large onions, minced

2 tablespoons chicken fat

Grieben (quantity to taste)

4 large or 6 medium-size potatoes, boiled and mashed

1 egg

Freshly ground pepper and herbal seasoning to taste

Sauté the onions in the chicken fat until golden. In a wooden bowl, chop the grieben. Add the hot mashed potatoes, sautéed onions, egg, and seasonings. Mix well to blend ingredients and the filling is ready to use.

POTATO FILLING (MILCHIG):

Follow the same recipe as above but substitute butter for the chicken fat and omit the grieben. Chop some soy nuts in the wooden bowl in place of the grieben and proceed as above. Recent research reveals that soy products may play an important role in the fight against cancer and heart disease. Soy nuts are also a source of lecithin, which emulsifies cholesterol, thus minimizing arterial plaque build-up.

CHEESE FILLING (NONSWEET):

2 tablespoons unsalted butter

1 large onion, diced

1 pound farmer, pot, ricotta, or cottage cheese

¼ cup wheat germ

2 eggs (if using cottage cheese, use only 1 egg)

In a skillet, melt the butter. Add the diced onion and sauté lightly. In a bowl, combine the cheese, wheat germ, and eggs. Add the sautéed onion. Combine well and the filling is ready to use.

CHEESE AND RAISIN FILLING:

1 pound cottage cheese

1 egg

2 tablespoons wheat germ

1 tablespoon soy grits (optional)

1½ teaspoons lemon rind

¼ teaspoon ground cinnamon

1 tablespoon honey

½ cup raisins

1 tablespoon yogurt or sour cream

In a large bowl, combine all ingredients. Mix well and the filling is ready to use.

Kasha—roasted buckwheat—is not really a grain, although it cooks up like a grain. It is an honored member of the rhubarb family. Kasha is rich

KASHA FILLING:

1 cup kasha (buckwheat groats)

1 egg

2 cups boiling water

1 teaspoon herbal seasoning

2 onions

Butter, oil, or chicken fat

In a bowl, combine the kasha and egg. Place the mixture in a hot dry skillet, stirring until the kernels are separated and toasted. Add the boiling water and the seasoning. Cover and cook over low heat for about 40 minutes.

Meanwhile, mince the onions and sauté in butter, oil, or chicken fat. Add to the kasha and the filling is ready to use.

in iron, contains almost all the B vitamins, is a good source of calcium, and is considered a curative plant because of its high content of rutin, a bioflavonoid that combats capillary fragility. Many physicians prescribe rutin for circulatory problems, varicosities, and hemorrhoids. It's nice to know that a dish so tasty can do so many good things for you.

More Tasty Blintzes

In Chapter Seven, I offer you a wonderful recipe for cheese blintzes for Shavuot (or any time). Use the Very Thin Blintz Blanket recipe on page 94 to prepare these tasty blintz variations.

POTATO BLINTZES

These are favored by all the men in our family. They are more robust than the cheese and very tasty. They can be dairy, pareve, or fleishig depending on the fat you use. (I'm talking about the blintzes, not the men.)

2 eggs

6 medium-size unpeeled potatoes, scrubbed, boiled, and mashed

2 tablespoons wheat germ

Freshly ground pepper and herbal seasoning to taste

2 medium-size onions, finely chopped

Butter, canola oil, or chicken fat

In a mixing bowl or food processor, blend the eggs, potatoes, wheat germ, and seasoning. Sauté the onions in butter for dairy, oil for pareve, and chicken fat (you should be so lucky!) for fleishig. Add the onions to the potato mixture and the filling is ready to use.

Yield: enough filling for approximately 20 blintzes

Note: In order to distinguish the potato from the cheese blintzes, I roll the potato blintzes but do not tuck in the ends. This guarantees that the potato-lovers will not be disappointed when they dig in.

Fleishig Blintzes

A meat-meal specialty.

3 cups chopped cooked meat or chicken

1 egg plus 1 egg yolk

¼ teaspoon freshly ground pepper

3 tablespoons chicken gravy or stock

Combine all ingredients and the filling is ready to use.

Yield: enough filling for approximately 20 blintzes

Blueberry Dessert Blintzes

Keep a supply in your freezer and you're always ready for company.

2 cups fresh blueberries

½ teaspoon ground cinnamon

½ teasoon almond extract

2 tablespoons arrowroot starch or cornstarch

½ cup chopped nuts or sunflower seeds (optional)

2 tablespoons honey

Combine all ingredients and the filling is ready to use.

Yield: enough filling for about 20 blintzes

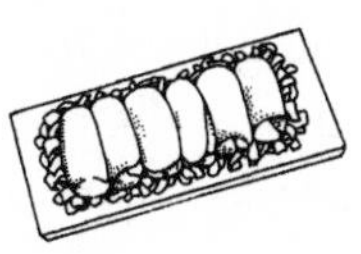

13

Make a Little Meat Go a Long Way

Meat on the table used to be a sign of good times or special occasions. But the pendulum has swung. Meat is no longer considered the indispensable food for the good life. And certainly, for good health one should take the emphasis off meat.

To cut down on meat without giving it up, learn how to stretch it. By doing so, you will be reducing your potential for cancer and heart disease and enjoy more fiber and flavor.

The method of preparation most amenable to stretching is stir-frying. That's fine because you can make stir-fries in endless variety using a little meat and lots of vegetables and grains. When trying to stretch, use chopped meat in different guises and you'll never get a complaint. "Chopped meat" can be ground lamb, veal, beef, chicken, or turkey and can be further enriched by the addition of organ meat, which is far more nutritious than muscle meat.

My butcher, who has been in cahoots with me for years, adds heart to my chuck for my special hamburger mix: one part heart to two parts chuck. It makes a juicy, tasty mixture which my children loved and so did their friends who came for homework and stayed for dinner. I must confess that I never told them what was in it. Many people have an emotional hangup when it comes to eating organ meats. So don't tell them. Just smile, because you know that when you add heart to your hamburger, you greatly reduce the fat, improve the quality of the protein, increase the vitamins, and lower the calories. Chuck loads you up with ten times more fat than heart, half as much iron, and half as much vitamin A. Heart is also much richer in the B vitamins. Add up all these values and you realize that heart is much better for your heart.

The dishes you prepare from the following recipes will win plaudits from your family and will stimulate some creative combinations of your own.

BEEF HEART CHOW

Try this very lowfat, highly nutritious recipe for sweet-and-sour heart. It's delicious with kasha varnishkes or mamaligge (cornmeal mush).

2 veal hearts

2 tablespoons canola oil or chicken fat

1½ cups tomato chunks

¼ cup vegetable broth, chicken broth, or water

¼ cup cider vinegar, or to taste

¼ cup honey, or to taste

2 tablespoons whole-wheat flour or arrowroot starch

3 tablespoons water

2 tablespoons lecithin granules (optional)

¼ teaspoon paprika

Trim away the gristle and cut the hearts into cubes. Heat the oil or chicken fat in a heavy pot that has a good-fitting lid.

Lightly sauté the hearts over moderate heat for 5 minutes. Add the tomato and broth or water. Add the vinegar and honey. Cover and simmer for about 40 minutes or until the heart is fork-tender.

Mix the flour or arrowroot with the 3 tablespoons of water and add this mixture to the heart mixture. Cook and stir until the gravy thickens. Add the lecithin and paprika.

Yield: 8 very nice servings

VEAL FRICASSEE

2 pounds veal, cut into 1-inch cubes

4 tablespoons soy flour

2 tablespoons canola oil or chicken fat

1 teaspoon powdered kelp

½ teaspoon freshly ground pepper, or to taste

1 onion, sliced

1 cup celery, cut into 1-inch pieces

1 cup fresh or frozen peas

1 tablespoon nutritional yeast (optional)

1 cup tomato juice

Enjoy this appetizing dish in good health. The meat is dredged in soy flour, which contributes genistein, a substance that has been found to inhibit a wide variety of cancer cells.

Dredge the veal cubes in the soy flour. In a large heavy pot, heat the oil and brown the veal cubes on all sides. Add the kelp, pepper, onion, celery, and peas. Stir the nutritional yeast into the tomato juice and pour into the veal pot. Cover and simmer for about 1 hour, until the veal is tender. Serve with mashed potatoes or brown rice.

Yield: 6 servings

Microwave Method: After browning the veal cubes, combine all ingredients in a 2-quart microwave-safe pot and cook on high, tightly covered, for 15 minutes. Remove from the oven, uncover, and stir. Taste-check the seasoning before serving.

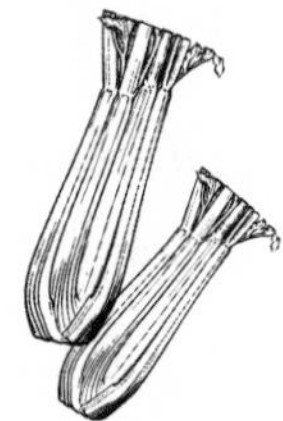

STUFFED CABBAGE (Holopches)

It is customary to serve this cabbage dish during the festival of Sukkot because of the ease with which it can be carried to the Sukkah. This recipe captures the spirit and appetizing aroma of Grandma's kitchen, but provides extra nutritional benefits.

There is another very good reason for enjoying cabbage, not only on Sukkot but many times throughout the year. Cabbage is the king of the cancer-fighting crucifer family, which some studies have shown to reduce the risk of gastrointestinal and respiratory tract cancers.

1 large head of cabbage (4 to 5 pounds)

Water

1 pound ground meat (¾ pound chuck and ¼ pound heart, if possible)

2 tablespoons wheat germ

1 garlic clove, minced

2 eggs

2 onions, grated

Powdered kelp or salt and freshly ground pepper

½ cup raw brown rice

1 can (28 ounces) **tomatoes**

2 onions, sliced

Meat bones or a few lamb riblets (optional)

2 tablespoons honey, or to taste

Juice of 1 lemon

2 bay leaves

1 tart apple, quartered

Using a sharp knife, remove the core from the cabbage. (Chew on it while you prepare the dish: it contains some excellent nutrients!)

Fill a pot large enough to accommodate the cabbage about half full with water. Bring to a boil. Place the cabbage in the boiling water; boil for a few minutes, then remove the cabbage. With a fork, remove the leaves and return to the water to soften a little. Turn off the heat. Now prepare the filling.

Combine the meat, wheat germ, garlic, eggs, onions, seasonings, and rice. Mix well. Lay out the cabbage leaves and cut off the hard part. Put a heaping tablespoon of filling on each leaf. Roll up like a blintz.

In a heavy pot like a Dutch oven, or in a roaster, mix the tomatoes, sliced onions and the meat bones or lamb riblets, if you're using them. Put any remaining odds and ends of cabbage in, too. Lay the cabbage rolls in gently, seam side down. Cover the pot and bring to a boil. Lower the heat and cook for 1 hour. Add the honey, lemon juice, bay leaves and apple. Continue to cook for 45 minutes more. Taste-check for seasoning. Add more honey or lemon juice if needed.

This dish can also be baked in a preheated 350-degree F. oven for about 2 hours. It freezes well. When you reheat, you may have to add some tomato sauce. Heat it gently to avoid burning.

Yield: 6 servings as a main dish, 10 to 12 as an appetizer

Microwave Method: Combine all ingredients as above in a microwave-safe casserole. Cover with vented microsafe plastic wrap. Microcook on high for 12 minutes or until bubbly. Turn the cabbage rolls over so they cook evenly. Reduce the power to medium and microcook for 25 minutes longer or until tender. Let stand for about 10 minutes.

Poultry Variation: Use ground cooked chicken or turkey instead of the chopped meat.

Reduced-meat or Meatless Variation: To cut down further on the meat, substitute crumbled tofu for half the meat. Or make the dish vegetarian by eliminating the meat and using all tofu.

A Balebusta Uses Brains

When I ask my butcher if he has any brains, he usually says, "If I had any brains, would I be a butcher? Maybe next week I will find a calf with some brains. I'll save them for you."

If you're smart, you'll use brains. They provide protein of a superior quality and are one of the richest sources of the B vitamin choline, which plays an important role in the way you utilize cholesterol and, according to recent research, has a direct effect on brain function and on memory.

I concede that many people, even members of my family, recoil at the idea of eating brains. So I cook the brains in soup, then I purée them with some of the soup in the blender and watch with secret glee as they spoon the soup down, getting smarter with every mouthful. There are many ways to fix brains, ways that hide their identity but don't disguise their virtues.

How to Precook Brains

Many recipes call for precooked brains. Whether you use calf, lamb, or cow brains, the cooking method is the same. Put them in a saucepan with cold water to cover. Add 2 tablespoons of vinegar. Cook for 25 minutes over moderate heat. Remove from the water, cool slightly, then remove the membrane.

Microwave Method: Place the brains rounded side up in a 2-quart microwave-safe dish. Combine ½ cup water with 2 tablespoons vinegar and pour over the brains. Cover tightly and cook on high for 4 minutes. Uncover, turn over the brains, re-cover, and cook for another 4 minutes. They're now ready to go into soup or to be used in the following recipes. No need to struggle with the outer membrane, it dissolves in the microwave oven.

Brain Fritters

Mom called them "smart latkes" and served them for breakfast whenever we were scheduled for exams. She was right on target!

2 eggs
⅓ cup whole-wheat or soy flour
3 tablespoons cold water
¼ teaspoon paprika
¼ teaspoon powdered kelp
⅛ teaspoon freshly ground pepper
1 set cooked brains
Canola, peanut, or olive oil

In a bowl, beat the eggs. Stir in the flour and water to make a batter. Add the seasonings and mix. Slice the brains and dip the slices into the batter. Sauté in hot oil until browned.

Yield: 4 servings

Brains Vinaigrette

Smooth, rich, and savory.

⅓ cup wine vinegar
⅓ cup olive oil
¼ teaspoon prepared mustard
1 teaspoon reduced-sodium soy sauce
1 set cooked brains
1 hard-cooked egg, finely chopped
1 teaspoon chopped fresh dill
1 teaspoon chopped fresh chives

Prepare a marinade of equal parts wine vinegar and olive oil; stir in the mustard; add the soy sauce. Slice the brains and marinate them for several hours. Serve slighly chilled. Sprinkle with the chopped egg , dill, and chives just before serving.

Yield: 4 servings

Sweetbreads

Sweetbreads are not a confection. They are the thymus gland of the calf. They are extremely perishable, so use them right away after purchase or freeze them.

Prepare sweetbreads the same way as brains—preferably by microwaving. There will be less cleaning, blanching, firming, and struggling with the membrane, which is dissolved in the microwave.

1 pound sweetbreads

1 cup liquid

Combine the sweetbreads and liquid in a 2-quart dish. Cover tightly and microcook on high for 5 minutes.

SWEETBREADS AND MUSHROOMS

This is the delicate dish served at lavish weddings. The sweetbreads and mushrooms are a Fountain of Youth duo, rich in nucleic acids, which help your cells stay young longer. The thymus gland enhances immune potential, and recently, at the Weizmann Institute

1 tablespoon canola oil or chicken fat

1 cup sliced mushrooms

5 tablespoons whole-wheat flour

2 cups vegetable or chicken stock

2 teaspoons reduced-sodium soy sauce

1/4 teaspoon freshly ground pepper

1/4 teaspoon onion powder

1 pound cooked sweetbreads

1 cup mung bean sprouts or 1 cup peas (canned or frozen)

Patty shells, cooked brown rice, or whole-grain toast

In a deep skillet, heat the oil and brown the mushrooms. Stir in the flour. Add the liquid slowly, then the soy sauce and seasonings. Cook for about 5 minutes over medium heat until thickened, stirring constantly.

in Israel, it was found to combat dangerous infections in children.

❧

Break the sweetbreads into small pieces and add to the mushrooms. Add the sprouts or peas and heat through. Serve in patty shells or over brown rice or whole-grain toast.

Yield: 6 to 8 elegant servings

More Tasty Meat Dishes

Beef Tongue with Raisins

This is a must at every one of our family festivities. It can be served hot or cold, which makes it lovely for Shabbat meals or for snacking.

❧

1 beef tongue (about 3 pounds)

Cold water

1 cup raisins

1 cup prune juice

1 cup water

In a large Dutch oven or heavy pot, place the tongue. Add cold water to cover. Cook for 3 hours or until tender. Remove the skin from the tongue.

Place the skinned tongue in an ovenproof pan. Add the raisins, prune juice, and water. Place in a 350-degree F. oven and bake for 1 hour, basting frequently with the pan juices. Slice and serve with or without sauce between two slices of challah spread with a little mustard.

Yield: 8 to 10 servings

Microwave Note: Fresh tongue does better in the conventional oven. Smoked tongue does well in the microwave and is cooked on high for about 20 minutes.

LIVER STEAK

Some people turn up their noses at the idea of eating liver. They don't know what they're missing. Not only is liver low in fat, it is a goldmine of the antioxidant vitamin A. It is rich in choline and inositol, which help you utilize cholesterol, and in lecithin, which helps you remember where you put your glasses.

Your success with liver depends on how you prepare it. Do not overcook and do not use high heat. If it's tough, you've probably cooked it too long.

1 tablespoon chicken fat or canola, peanut, or olive oil

1 medium-size onion, diced

1 cup sliced mushrooms

Lemon juice

1 pound baby beef liver, washed and briefly broiled on both sides

2 tablespoons sesame seeds

1 tablespoon wheat germ or bran

1 tablespoon herbal seasoning or the seasonings of your choice

In a heavy skillet, heat the chicken fat or oil and sauté the onion and mushrooms.

Meantime, sprinkle lemon juice on the liver and coat it with sesame seeds, wheat germ or bran, and seasonings.

Remove the sautéed onions and mushrooms. Add a little more fat to the skillet if it needs it, put the liver in and sauté briefly on each side or until it is pink, not red, when you cut it. Serve with applesauce, a green vegetable, and a crunchy baked potato.

Yield: 4 servings

Chopped Liver

1 pound lamb or baby beef liver or 8 chicken livers, broiled

½ medium-size onion, diced

Chicken skin and chicken fat

3 crisp lettuce leaves

2 hard-cooked eggs

1 tablespoon chicken fat

Cut up the liver into a wooden chopping bowl. Add whatever sautéed onions you have on hand or sauté the diced onion with a few pieces of chicken skin and chicken fat. Remove the onions when they are nice and crisp and let the chicken skin crisp up. The resulting pieces of grieben are sheer magic in chopped liver. When they are crisp, add them to the chopping bowl. A good substitute for grieben is soy nuts, the roasted ones you get in natural food stores. The soy also contributes lecithin, a nice little bundle of vitamins and genistein, the magic ingredient in soy products shown to prevent cancer.

Add a few lettuce leaves (they contribute moistness, lessening the need for added fat) and the hard-cooked eggs and chop away. When chopped to the desired consistency, mix in the tablespoon of chicken fat.

Serve as a salad with grated white radish or spread on whole-grain crackers, matzo, or on challah for a yummy sandwich.

Yield: about 2 cups of chopped liver

Remember that, to be kosher, liver must always be broiled before it is used in any way. After it is broiled, it may be used in other ways. First wash the liver, then broil under the flame on a wire rack so the blood drips off into the drip pan.

I always prepare more liver than we need for dinner. Next day we have chopped liver as a salad or as an hors d'oeuvre. If you don't have any leftover liver and you want chopped liver, use the following recipe.

PITCHA (Calves'-foot Jelly)

Some like it hot; some like it cold. It's delicious either way. Served hot on a bleak wintry day, there's nothing like it for making you feel like June in January. You can almost feel its strength bringing new vigor to your bones and vital organs.

You will need calves' feet, which your friendly butcher will provide, all washed and chopped. If he doesn't have feeselach (feet), settle for shin bones.

2 feeselach (more if you're lucky)
Cold water
1 or 2 onions, minced
2 or 3 garlic cloves, to taste, minced
2 tablespoons vinegar
2 bay leaves, crushed
Hard-cooked eggs for cold pitcha
1 raw egg for hot pitcha
Juice of 1 lemon for hot pitcha
Toasted challah rubbed with garlic for hot pitcha
Garlic cloves, minced

Make sure the feeselach are clean, then put them in a pot with cold water to cover by 2 inches. Bring to a boil and skim off the foam. Add the onion, garlic, vinegar, and bay leaves. Cook over low heat for about 3 hours—until the meat separates easily from the bones. Add more water if necessary.

For cold pitcha, remove the feet from the pot. Remove the meat from the feet and cut it into small pieces into a nonaluminum loaf pan. Strain the liquid from the pot over the cut-up meat. Add slices of hard-cooked eggs. Or, do like my Mom used to do: bury whole hard-cooked eggs in the mixture.

Either way, chill the mixture. It will jell and become solid. Serve it with a cruet of vinegar on the side. We served it this way at one of our Bar Mitzvah celebrations and it made a hit. Everyone had a story about how "Mamma used to make it."

For hot pitcha, after the initial cooking period, beat up an egg, add the lemon juice, and beat well. Add a tablespoon of the hot liquid and continue beating to blend the ingredients. Add this mixture to the pot, mixing well to prevent curdling.

To serve, toast day-old bread or challah—a slice for each person—in the oven until crispy. Rub both sides with garlic. Put a piece of garlic toast in each bowl. Serve the bones and liquid broth on top. *Es gezunte hait.*

Yield: 6 to 8 servings, depending on how many feeselach you use

Ruthie's Karnatzlach

Dismayed by the artificial colors and nitrites in hot dogs, beloved food of children, my daughter serves karnatzlach instead. She makes a spicy hamburger mixture and shapes it to resemble hot dogs.

1½ pounds ground meat mixture (chuck or neck with heart, if possible)

1 onion, grated

1 large carrot, grated

1 garlic clove, minced

3 tablespoons soy or whole-wheat flour

Pinch of crushed dried thyme, marjoram, and oregano or 2 teaspoons poultry seasoning

2 eggs, lightly beaten

Dash of powdered kelp

⅓ cup wheat germ

½ teaspoon paprika

3 tablespoons sesame seeds

Hot tomato sauce

In a bowl, combine the meat, onion, carrot, garlic, flour, seasonings, and eggs. Mix well and form into rolls about the diameter of a frankfurter and about 3 inches long, tapering at both ends. Roll each in a mixture of kelp, wheat germ, paprika, and sesame seeds. Broil under moderate heat on a lightly oiled rack. Turn to brown on all sides. Serve with hot tomato sauce.

Yield: 24 karnatzlach, 8 servings

Variation: Use this recipe to make a nutrition-packed meatloaf.

CHOLENT

Cholent is a meal-in-one stew. During the long cooking time, the flavors of the barley, beans, potato, and meat blend, forming a flavorsome repast.

Traditionally, cholent cooks all Friday night and is enjoyed by the entire family after attending synagogue services on Saturday. There is a theory that the word cholent *is a contraction of the words* Shule ende

1 cup cranberry beans

1 cup navy beans

Water

1 medium-size onion, cut up

1 tablespoon canola or olive oil or chicken fat

Several marrow bones

1 pound chuck or brisket, cut into 2-inch chunks

1 cup barley

Ground pepper, powdered kelp, and herbal seasoning to taste

1 teaspoon paprika

3 unpeeled potatoes, scrubbed and quartered

Soak the beans overnight in water. (If you forgot to soak them, cover with water, bring to a boil, remove from the heat, and allow to soak for about 1 hour.)

In a large heavy pot, simmer the onion in the oil or fat. Add the bones and meat, the drained beans, the barley, and the seasonings. Cover liberally with water and simmer for 1 hour.

Add the potatoes and cook slowly for 30 minutes more. Taste-check for seasoning. Add water to 3 inches above the contents of the pot. Cover tightly and place in a preheated 225-degree F. oven overnight. You'll have a nice hot dish at noon.

Yield: 6 servings

(synagogue services have ended), and that means it's time to eat!

GOULASH

A hearty economical dish that fills the house with an appetizing aroma. The lecithin emulsifies the fat, thus lowering the cholesterol levels of the beef. This dish seems to do better in the conventional oven than in the microwave.

1 tablespoon chicken fat or canola, peanut, or olive oil
2 small onions, sliced
1 garlic clove, minced
1½ pounds stewing beef, cubed
1 cup cooked or canned tomatoes, cut up
2 tablespoons lecithin granules
1 cup water or stock
1 teaspoon paprika
½ teaspoon powdered kelp
3 medium-size unpeeled potatoes, scrubbed

In a skillet, heat the chicken fat or oil and sauté the onions and garlic until golden. In a pot, combine the beef, tomatoes, lecithin, and water or stock. Add the sautéed onion and garlic. Then add the paprika and kelp. Cover and cook in a 350-degree F. oven for 1 hour. Slice the potatoes lengthwise, add to the stew and simmer for another 30 minutes. Taste-check and adjust the seasoning.

Yield: 6 servings

14

Fish Dishes
(A Valentine for Your Heart)

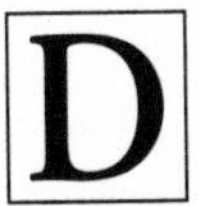

o your heart a favor while you pleasure your palate. Eat more fish. Fish and fish oils have been shown to make both cholesterol and triglycerides do a nosedive.

Studies published in the *New England Journal of Medicine* demonstrate that the special Omega-3 fatty acids in fish can unclog arteries, make the blood less prone to clotting, and have a positive effect on inflammatory diseases. "These highly unsaturated fats seem to give benefit in every study we've reviewed," says William Castelli, M.D., director of the Framingham Heart Study.

Fish has its merits for everyone. But, for those who wish to cut calories without sacrificing nutrients, fish is definitely a top-of-the-barrel catch. At approximately 100 calories in three ounces, fish is an attractive alternative to the 330 calories in an equivalent amount of meat.

It may surprise you to know that fish is low in sodium, even the fish that swim around in the salty ocean. Fish also provides calcium in a form that the body utilizes well. The calcium-phosphorus ratio corresponds roughly to that of milk. If your kids won't drink their milk, or if they are lactose intolerant, let them eat fish.

Fish also contributes to your stores of iron and is an excellent source of copper, a mineral that is scarce in the usual diet but one that is necessary for making hemoglobin out of iron. Fish is also a marvelous source of iodine, so necessary to the proper functioning of the thyroid gland.

Here are some great recipes to give fish top priority at your table.

FILLETS OF SOLE WITH DILLED CUCUMBER

I like to keep a supply of sole fillets in the freezer ready for drop-in company. It's quick, easy, very low in calories, and, as my kids say, "It just hits the spot."

4 fillets of sole or other fish (approximately 1½ pounds)

1 to 2 teaspoons olive, canola, or sesame oil

Freshly ground pepper

Snipped fresh dill weed

2 medium-size cucumbers, sliced thin

4 teaspoons lemon juice

Paprika, parsley sprigs, and lemon wedges for garnish

Arrange the fillets in a baking dish. Put a few drops of oil on top of each, then sprinkle with pepper and dill. Cover the fillets with cucumber slices, then sprinkle more pepper and dill on top of each.

Cover the baking dish tightly. Bake at 325 degrees F. for 12 to 15 minutes. Remove from the oven and uncover the dish. Sprinkle each piece of fish with a teaspoon of lemon juice, then sprinkle with paprika and garnish with parsley sprigs and lemon wedges.

Yield: 4 servings

Fish Gumbo with Tomatoes and Bananas

An unusual combination—but a delicious one. The bananas provide a sweet and smooth counterpoint to the tartness of the tomatoes.

1 tablespoon unsalted butter or canola or olive oil

½ cup finely chopped onion

½ green pepper, finely sliced (membrane and seeds removed)

1 garlic clove, minced

1 tablespoon whole-wheat flour

2 cups vegetable broth or water

1 can (16 ounces) **tomatoes**

⅓ cup chopped parsley

1 bay leaf

¼ teaspoon crushed dried thyme

⅛ teaspoon freshly ground pepper

2 pounds fish fillets, cut into 2-inch chunks

1 cup thinly sliced carrots, zucchini, or broccoli

1 teaspoon lemon juice

1 teaspoon reduced-sodium soy sauce

⅛ teapoon cayenne pepper

4 medium-size bananas, cut into 1½-inch chunks

3 cups hot cooked brown rice

In a large deep skillet, heat the butter or oil. Add the onion, green pepper, and garlic. Cook for about 5 minutes, until the vegetables are soft. Add the flour and cook for 2 minutes, stirring constantly.

While stirring, pour in the broth or water. Add the tomatoes, parsley, bay leaf, thyme, and pepper. Bring to a boil, reduce the heat and let simmer, partially covered, for 20 minutes.

Add the fish and your choice of vegetable and simmer for 10 more minutes. Discard the bay leaf. Stir in the lemon juice, soy sauce, cayenne, and bananas. Serve immediately over hot brown rice.

Microwave Method: Omit the fat. In an uncovered 4-quart microwave-safe casserole, microcook the onion, pepper, and garlic with 1 tablespoon of broth or water on high for about 2 minutes. Stir in the flour. Add only 1½ cups more of broth or water, the tomatoes, parsley, bay leaf, thyme, and pepper. Microcook for 8 minutes. Add the fish and the carrots, zucchini, or broccoli. Microwave, covered with vented plastic wrap, on high for 4 minutes. Discard the bay leaf. Stir in the lemon juice, soy sauce, cayenne, and bananas. Serve over the hot brown rice.

Yield: **6 servings**

MUSTARD-FLAVORED FISH FILLETS WITH ALMONDS

Quick, easy, and very tasty. They're baked in the oven but they're so crunchy you'll think they're fried.

4 fish fillets (approximately 1½ pounds)
Freshly ground pepper to taste
2 tablespoons Dijon mustard
2 tablespoons unsalted butter, softened
½ cup toasted wheat germ combined with ½ cup toasted bread crumbs
½ cup sliced or slivered almonds, toasted
½ cup plain yogurt or reduced-fat sour cream
1 tablespoon reduced-fat mayonnaise
Parsley sprigs for garnish

Preheat the oven to 425 degrees F. Grease a shallow medium-size ovenproof casserole with nonstick baking spray.

Place the fish in the casserole in a single layer and sprinkle with pepper. Mix the mustard with 1 tablespoon of the butter and, using a small spatula or butter knife, spread it on the surface of fish. Bake for about 7 minutes, or until the fish flakes easily.

Meanwhile, melt the remaining butter and toss with the combined wheat germ and bread crumbs. Set aside. Combine the almonds with the yogurt or sour cream and the mayonnaise. Remove the fish and spread the almond-yogurt mixture over it. Broil for 2 minutes. Remove and pile the wheat germ and bread crumb mixture on top. Return to the broiler for a few seconds more or just long enough to brown the crumbs. Watch it carefully lest it burn. Garnish with parsley sprigs.

Yield: 4 servings

Baked Cod in Parchment

The parchment packages steam the cod and accompanying vegetables in their own flavorful juices, preserving the nutrients and minimizing the need for added fat.

1 tablespoon olive or canola oil

3 shallots or scallions, sliced

2 medium-size zucchini, sliced

2 large carrots, sliced

1 medium-size red bell pepper, sliced

¼ cup chopped fresh basil leaves or 1 teaspoon dried

½ teaspoon herbal seasoning

¼ teaspoon freshly ground pepper

4 cod fillets (approximately 5 ounces each)

In a skillet, heat the oil; add the shallots or scallions and sauté for 3 minutes. Add the zucchini, carrots, and pepper and sauté for 3 to 4 minutes or until crisp-tender. Stir in the basil and other seasonings.

Preheat the oven to 400 degrees F. Cut out 4 fourteen-inch rounds of parchment paper or aluminum foil. Place each fillet a little off-center on a parchment round. Spoon the vegetable mixture over the fillets. Fold over the parchment so the edges meet and the fish is in the center of the packet. Fold and crimp the edges to seal.

Transfer the packets to a baking sheet. Bake for 15 minutes. Serve the packets intact. Let the diners cut open their own packets and enjoy the lovely aromas.

Yield: 4 servings

POACHED SALMON

Whether it swims in the Atlantic or the Pacific, salmon is high in protein and in fat. But even the fattest has less fat than chicken or steak, and what fat it does have is unsaturated and a superior source of the wonder-working

2 quarts water

1 cup dry white wine

2 tablespoons peppercorns

1 tablespoon herbal seasoning

2 onions, sliced

½ cup white wine vinegar

1 cup chopped celery with leaves

Lemon slices

1 whole salmon (5 to 6 pounds or one that fits your poacher)

Put all ingredients except the salmon in the poacher. Bring to a boil and simmer for 5 minutes.

Wash the salmon; make sure all scales are removed, and trim off all of the fins. Check to see if the salmon fits your poacher. If it's a bit too long, trim off a little of the tail.

With a ruler, measure the thickest part of the fish and take note of it. Place the fish in the skimmer part of the poacher, or wrap the fish in cheesecloth to facilitate removal and place it in the poacher over high heat. When the court bouillon begins to boil, start timing the cooking. The salmon should cook for 10 minutes per inch of thickness. A 2-inch-thick fish should cook for 20 minutes. Figure another minute for every tenth of an inch more.

Remove the fish promptly to a warm platter. Carefully remove the cheesecloth if you used it. Serve with a Yogurt Dill Sauce *(see below)* on the side.

Yield: 10 servings

Omega-3 fatty acids.

Poached salmon is an elegant dish. It requires no additional fat and can be served hot or cold. The court bouillon that remains in the poacher can be refrigerated or frozen and used again.

YOGURT DILL SAUCE

1 cup plain yogurt

1 teaspoon grated onion

3 tablespoons minced fresh dill weed

1 teaspoon lemon juice

Combine all ingredients in a small glass bowl. The sauce is ready to use.

MOMMA'S GEFILTE FISH

Tradition lives! In Jewish homes all over the world, gefilte fish is a traditional Sabbath and holiday specialty.

Of course, some things change. You can now buy it in jars or cans, some with salt, some with sugar, some jelled, some with all white fish, some with a mixture of several kinds of fish. But there's nothing like the kind that Momma made, the kind you make yourself.

When selecting fish, consider varieties with different textures: fat, dry, and flaky. Traditional choices are carp, pike, white, and of course a little buffalo. Actually, what Momma called buffalo is a freshwater bass with a little mouth. I guess it has the visage of a buffalo. (It is not now generally available.)

3 pounds fish (carp, pike, or whiting)
2 onions, grated (reserve 2 pieces of onion skin)
2 carrots, grated
2 eggs, lightly beaten
2 teaspoons herbal seasoning
½ teaspoon freshly ground pepper
½ cup water
3 tablespoons ground almonds or whole-wheat bread crumbs
2 onions, sliced
2 carrots, sliced
2 cups water

Fillet the fish or have it filleted at the fish market. Retain the skin, bones, and heads. Using a grinder or food processor, purée the fish fillets. Remove to a mixing bowl. Add the grated onions, grated carrots, eggs, 1 teaspoon herbal seasoning, ¼ teaspoon pepper, ½ cup water, and the ground almonds or bread crumbs. Mix well to combine the ingredients. The mixture should feel just slightly sticky.

On the bottom of a large heavy pot or fish poacher, place the skin, bones, and heads. Add the sliced onions, sliced carrots, 2 cups water, 1 teaspoon herbal seasoning, the remaining ¼ teaspoon pepper, and the onion skins. Cover the pot, bring to a boil, then lower heat and simmer for about 20 minutes.

Meanwhile, with moistened hands, shape the fish into ovals about 3 inches long and 1¼ inches in diameter. Place them on wax paper. Bring the broth to a smiling roll and lower the fish into the broth. Make sure the boiling liquid almost covers the fish. If necessary, add another ½ cup of water. Lower the heat and simmer on a very low flame for 2 hours. Let cool in the broth.

Using a slotted spoon, remove the cooled fish to a serving dish. Remove the carrots from the broth and garnish each piece of fish with a slice of carrot.

Cook down the stock to concentrate it, adjust the seasoning, then spoon a little over the gefilte fish. Leave to "set," and serve cold with horseradish.

Yield: about 12 pieces

Polish-style gefilte fish calls for haddock, cod, or whiting. The haddock is desirable because it contributes a firmer texture. Adding the onion skins gives the broth a lovely color.

My Mom used carp, pike, whiting, and when she could find it, buffalo. (She called it buffel.)

This is Mom's recipe.

Salmon Gefilte Fish

Tastes like the kind you spend hours preparing. This version is very simple and quick to make and brings you the extra nutrients and polyunsaturates found in salmon. Serve it for a change on Shabbat or, as I do, on Sukkot.

4 onions

1 stalk celery with leaves

3 cups water

3 sprigs fresh parsley or 1 tablespoon dried parsley flakes

1 can (16 ounces) **pink salmon,** drained and mashed (reserve the liquid and include the calcium-rich bones and skin when you mash the salmon)

2 eggs, beaten

¼ teaspoon ground white pepper, or to taste

1 teaspoon powdered kelp or herbal seasoning

2 tablespoons wheat germ

2 parsnips

4 carrots

Slice 3 of the onions into a large soup pot. Add the celery, water, and parsley. Bring to a slow boil.

Put the salmon in a bowl and grate the remaining onion into it. Add the beaten eggs, pepper, kelp or herbal seasoning, and wheat germ. Blend the ingredients together and form into balls. Then flatten the balls slightly. Add a little matzo meal if necessary to hold them together.

Slice the parsnips and carrots, first in half, then lengthwise. Place them in the pot. Add the reserved salmon liquid, then the salmon balls. Cook, covered, for 30 minutes. Allow the fish balls to cool in the sauce.

Serve hot with tomato sauce or cold with horseradish. Ladle some of the sauce over each portion.

Yield: 12 portions

Halibut Fish Balls

This variation of gefilte fish can be made with different kinds of fish. Haddock or halibut give the fish a firmer texture. Don't forget the horseradish!

2 pounds halibut or haddock, or a combination

1 medium-size onion

2 eggs

3 tablespoons wheat germ or oat bran, or a combination

½ cup fish stock or water

Herbal seasoning and freshly ground pepper, to taste

1 large onion, sliced

1 large carrot, sliced

Additional fish stock or water

In a grinder or in the food processor using the steel blade, grind the fish with the medium-size onion. Process until the ingredients are well chopped but not puréed. Add the eggs, wheat germ or oat bran, fish stock or water, and seasonings. Process until the ingredients are well blended.

Place the large sliced onion and the sliced carrot in the bottom of a large pot. With moistened hands, form the fish mixture into "golf balls" and place them in the pot. Add fish stock or water to cover the fish. Cover the pot and cook over low heat for about 1½ hours or until the fish balls are tender.

Yield: 12 servings

Mediterranean Fish-and-Vegetable Stew

This hearty bone-warming meal-in-a-dish is rich in flavorful antioxidant nutrients and easy to prepare.

2 cans (1 pound each) **stewed tomatoes**

1 clove garlic, minced

1 bay leaf

1 teaspoon crushed dried basil

1 teaspoon crushed dried thyme

½ teaspoon fennel or cumin seeds

¼ teaspoon crushed red pepper flakes

½ teaspoon grated orange zest

2 medium-size potatoes, scrubbed and sliced ⅛-inch thick

2 large carrots, scrubbed and sliced ⅛-inch thick

1 pound fish fillets, fresh or frozen and thawed, cut into 2-inch chunks

1 package (10 ounces) **frozen green peas**

Grated Parmesan cheese (optional)

In large heavy soup pot or Dutch oven, combine the tomatoes, garlic, bay leaf, basil, thyme, fennel or cumin seeds, pepper flakes, and orange zest. Mix to blend. Add the potatoes and carrots; mix to blend. Cover and bring to a boil over medium heat. Reduce the heat and simmer 40 minutes, stirring occasionally, until the potatoes and carrots are fork-tender.

Add the fish and peas. Stir gently. Cover and simmer for 5 to 10 minutes, until the fish flakes easily. Remove the bay leaf. Ladle the stew into shallow soup bowls. Pass the Parmesan cheese separately.

Yield: 4 to 6 servings

JODI'S BROILED FISH WITH CHEESE TOPPING

Easy enough for hurry-up dinners, elegant enough for black-tie dinners. The fish remains moist and full-flavored. The topping is crusty and mellow, a perfect meld. Serve with steamed broccoli and a brown rice pilaf.

4 flounder, sole, or cod fillets or steaks (approximately 1½ pounds)

Paprika

2 tablespoons mayonnaise

2 tablespoons yogurt

1 tablespoon chopped capers

1 tablespoon chopped chives

1 tablespoon chopped fresh parsley

½ cup grated Cheddar cheese

1 egg white

Arrange the fish fillets or steaks in one layer in an ovenproof serving dish. Sprinkle with paprika and broil for 3 minutes.

Combine the mayonnaise, yogurt, capers, chives, parsley, and cheese. Beat the egg white until stiff and fold it into the mayonnaise mixture. Spread this mixture over the fish and broil for 5 to 10 minutes, until the topping is deliciously brown.

Yield: 4 servings

SEAFOOD LINGUINE

1 teaspoon olive or canola oil

1 teaspoon unsalted butter

2 medium-size tomatoes, cubed

2 green onions, sliced

4 cloves garlic, minced

½ cup chopped fresh parsley

12 ounces "It's Not Crab"

2 tablespoons lemon juice

2 tablespoons minced fresh thyme, or 1 teaspoon, dried

½ teaspoon freshly ground pepper

1 box (1 pound) **linguine,** cooked and drained

In a large nonstick skillet, heat the oil and butter. Gently sauté the tomatoes, onions, and garlic for about 2 minutes. Do not let the garlic brown. Stir in the parsley, fish, lemon juice, thyme, and pepper. Simmer for another 2 minutes. Stir in the cooked linguine. Enjoy hot or cold!

Yield: 8 servings

There are some products now available that taste like shellfish but are actually made from pollock, a fin fish. One of the brands available is called "It's Not Crab!—It's Kosher Fish." It is precooked and can be used in any recipe that calls for canned tuna. Conversely, you can use canned tuna for this linguine.

15

Tofu
The Pareve Wonder

id you ever dream of eating your fill of luscious blueberry cheesecake without a worry about calories, cholesterol, or chemicals—and after a chicken dinner yet?

Well, listen up! You can make luscious cheeseless cheesecake from tofu, a remarkable Oriental food that marries well with Jewish cuisine.

I have used tofu in kugels, blintzes, gefilte fish, hamburgers, karnatzlach, stuffed cabbage, and in terrific creamy desserts. I serve them with pride with never a worry about mixing meat and dairy.

Tofu is a natural wholesome alternative to the nondairy concoctions loaded with chemicals. It is derived from soybeans, which recent research reveals may play an important role in our fight against both cancer and heart disease. It is also a terrific food for waist-watchers: an eight-ounce portion provides 147 calories, as opposed to 648 calories in an equal amount of hamburger and 320 in an equal amount of eggs.

Try the recipes in this chapter—but don't stop there. Go creative! Freeze some tofu and it will have a different texture. Put a few frozen chunks in a jar of gefilte fish and let it marinate in the juices overnight. Eat it with horseradish and enjoy the taste and texture of gefilte fish.

Last Friday I blended a chunk of tofu with the potatoes for the Shabbos kugel. It was light in color and texture and very tasty. Last night we had stuffed cabbage. I put a few chunks of tofu in the pot, and darn if it didn't taste like chunks of meat.

Tofu has been dubbed "the food of a thousand flavors" because, like a chameleon takes on colors, so does tofu take on flavors. Every time you prepare a meal, ask yourself, "Can I put some tofu in this dish?" Usually the answer is a big "Yes" and you are on the road to better health and some delightful culinary adventures.

GARLIC-FLAVORED TOFU DIP OR SALAD DRESSING

Garlic has a long and venerable reputation for killing germs. The Russians use a garlic vapor in their hospitals and as an antibiotic. It is rich in potassium, low in sodium, and provides some B vitamins and the antioxidant vitamin C. You get all these brilliant benefits in this pungent appetizing dip which can, with a little water, be converted into a salad dressing.

1 pound (2 cakes) **tofu**

1 clove garlic, crushed

2 teaspoons prepared mustard

1 tablespoon sesame or olive oil

½ teaspoon chopped dill weed

2½ tablespoons lemon juice

1 tablespoon finely chopped onion

2 tablespoons reduced-sodium Tamari soy sauce

Purée all ingredients in a blender or food processor and you have a creamy dip that is kind to your waistline but tastes like a thousand calories. Serve in a pretty bowl surrounded by all kinds of vegetables in the raw.

To use as a salad dressing, simply thin it with a little water.

Yield: 2 cups

TOFU-TAHINA SPREAD

Tahina (sesame butter) contributes linoleic acid, important to the body's utilization of fats and also to a glowing complexion. Its delicate nutty

8 ounces (½ cake) **tofu**

2 tablespoons tahina

1 teaspoon reduced-sodium Tamari soy sauce

Garlic powder (optional)

Lemon juice (optional)

Place all ingredients in a small bowl. With a fork, mash and blend all ingredients. If you like, season with garlic powder and lemon juice. Spread on crackers, bread, or pita, or stuff into celery sticks.

Yield: 1 cup

flavor is a perfect counterpoint to the other ingredients in this zippy spread.

TOFU AND GROUND BEEF

½ pound ground beef

1 clove garlic, minced

3 tablespoons finely chopped scallion or onion

2 cups sliced fresh mushrooms

2 cups tofu, cut into ½-inch cubes

2 tablespoons reduced-sodium Tamari soy sauce

1 teaspoon honey

1 tablespoon arrowroot starch or cornstarch

½ cup water or stock

In a nonstick skillet, combine the meat, garlic, scallion or onion, and mushrooms and cook, stirring occasionally, until the meat changes color. Drain off the fat. Add the tofu, Tamari, and honey. Cover and cook slowly for 10 minutes. Stir the starch into the water or stock; add to the tofu and meat mixture. Cook over low heat until the mixture thickens.

Yield: 6 to 8 servings

This dish brings you the flavor of meat with half the calories and fat. It tastes beefy, yet is made with only a half-pound of ground beef. This is a lowfat, mineral-rich, high-protein dish that provides only 180 calories in a half-cup serving.

MARINTATED TOFU WITH VEGETABLES

The vegetables are crisp-tender in this delightful vegetarian dish that brings you the flavor of London broil minus the calories and fat.

1 pound (2 cakes) **tofu**
¼ cup reduced-sodium Tamari soy sauce
3 tablespoons canola or olive oil
2 tablespoons lemon juice
3 tablespoons pineapple juice
3 tablespoons wine vinegar
4 cloves garlic, minced
⅛ teaspoon freshly ground pepper
1 eggplant, cubed and lightly steamed
1 onion, sliced
3 medium-size green bell peppers, sliced
Several whole mushrooms
Cherry tomatoes

First press the tofu as follows: Cube it, and place the cubes on a towel on the counter. Place another towel on top. Place a cookie sheet over all; evenly distribute 3 pounds of weight on the cookie sheet (use jars of beans or water). Let stand for at least 10 minutes.

While the tofu is being pressed, make a marinade by combining, in a bowl, the Tamari, oil, lemon and pineapple juices, vinegar, garlic, and pepper. Add the pressed tofu to the marinade. Allow to marinate for at least 30 minutes. Just before cooking, add the vegetables to the marinade.

Transfer the contents of the marinade bowl to a shallow 12 x 16–inch pan and broil 4 inches below the heat source. Baste and turn twice. When the tofu appears crisp, it is ready to be enjoyed. Serve over cooked brown rice.

Yield: 8 to 10 servings

Tofu Stir-Fry with Walnuts

The walnuts contribute a rich share of protein, bone-building calcium, the antioxidant vitamin A, vitamin B, and a delightful texture contrast.

1 large onion, chopped
1 tablespoon sesame, olive, or canola oil
4 large mushrooms, sliced
1 cup string beans, cut into 1-inch pieces
1 teaspoon powdered ginger
1 tablespoon finely chopped fresh ginger (optional)
1 large clove garlic, crushed
1½ tablespoons arrowroot starch or cornstarch
⅔ cup water
2 tablespoons reduced-sodium Tamari soy sauce
1 tablespoon wine or cider vinegar
1 teaspoon honey
1 pound tofu (2 cakes), cut into 1-inch cubes
½ cup chopped walnuts
Chopped fresh parsley

In a heavy skillet or in a wok, sauté the onion in the oil over medium heat for 1 minute. Add the sliced mushrooms and string beans (any vegetable may be substituted). Cover the pan and steam for 5 minutes. Add the ginger and garlic. Combine the starch and water and add to the pot. Add the soy sauce, vinegar, and honey.

Turn up the heat and stir vigorously as you bring the mixture to a boil. Then lower the heat to a simmer and add the tofu and walnuts. Simmer for a few minutes, until the sauce thickens. Garnish with parsley.

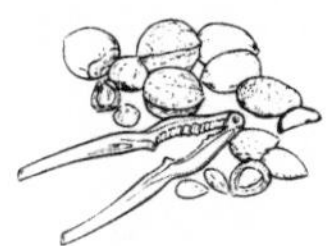

Serve as is or over cooked brown rice or cooked pasta. A delight to the eyes and the palate.

Yield: 4 servings

TOFU AMBROSIA

A creamy versatile dessert that can be served with meat or dairy. It's extremely high in protein and a powerhouse of the minerals that strengthen bones and come to the aid of your heart muscle.

1 cup orange juice

2 tablespoons honey

1 tablespoon arrowroot starch or cornstarch

1 tablespoon grated orange zest

3 drops almond extract

¾ pound (1½ cakes) **tofu,** drained and cut into ½-inch cubes

2 oranges or tangerines, sectioned and pitted

2 tablespoons unsweetened coconut flakes

2 tablespoons sliced almonds, lightly toasted

Reserve 2 tablespoons of the orange juice and combine the remaining juice and honey in a small saucepan. Heat gently to a simmer. Meanwhile, dissolve the starch in the 2 tablespoons of orange juice and add to the saucepan, stirring until the mixture thickens—about 30 seconds. Add the grated orange zest and the almond extract and stir to blend.

Combine the tofu and orange or tangerine sections in a glass bowl. Add the orange juice mixture and the coconut; stir gently to blend. Cover and chill for at least 1 hour.

Serve in attractive stemware or parfait glasses. Garnish with the toasted almonds.

Yield: 4 servings

Creamy Carob-Tofu Pie

For lovers of chocolate cream pie, here's a taste-alike with a big nutritional difference. It's low in fat, extremely low in calories, high in protein and life-enhancing minerals and free of additives.

FILLING:

1 cup dairy milk or cashew milk (⅓ cup cashews blended with ⅔ cup water)

2 pounds (4 cakes) **tofu**

½ cup pure maple syrup or honey

3 teaspoons vanilla extract

½ teaspoon ground cinnamon

½ cup carob powder

½ cup chopped walnuts or unsweetened coconut flakes

In a blender or food processor, combine all ingredients except the walnuts or coconut. Blend at high speed. Now stir in the walnuts or coconut. Set aside while you make the pie crust.

PIE CRUST:

1 cup whole-wheat pastry flour

⅓ cup unsalted butter or canola oil

4 tablespoons ice water

Place the flour in a bowl. Cut in the butter or add the oil and combine well. Add the water 1 tablespoon at a time until the dough forms a ball and leaves the sides of the bowl.

Roll out and place in a 10-inch pie plate. Flute the edge. Pour in the filling and bake for 13 minutes. Let cool, then chill or freeze before serving.

Yield: 8 servings

TOFU CHEESELESS "CHEESECAKE"

Enjoy a "cheesecake" splurge that's a weight-watcher's delight though it tastes like a zillion calories. This cake contains no cheese but it has a creamy consistency reminiscent of Lindy's.

FILLING:

1 cup raisins

½ cup apple juice

2 teaspoons grated lemon rind

3 tablespoons tahina (sesame butter)

1 tablespoon vanilla extract

4 pounds (8 cakes) **tofu**

3 tablespoons lemon juice

½ cup honey

Soak the raisins in the apple juice until soft—about 2 hours—or cook for 2 minutes on medium in the microwave. In a blender or food processor, purée the raisins with the apple juice and lemon rind. Remove this mixture from the blender or food processor and whiz the rest of the ingredients to make a tofu purée. You might have to do this in several batches. Combine the two purées and stir thoroughly. Set aside while you prepare the crust.

CRUST:

½ cup sunflower seeds or raw cashews, ground

½ cup wheat germ

2 teaspoons honey

½ teaspoon ground cinnamon

¼ teaspoon ground allspice

In a medium-size bowl, combine all ingredients and knead with your fingers until the mixture feels crumbly. Pat the mixture into a 9-inch springform pan, covering the bottom and about 1½ inches up the sides. Now spoon in the filling.

Place in a preheated 350-degree F. oven and bake for 25 to 30 minutes, until the top begins to brown delicately. Remove from the oven and allow to cool. Using a knife, separate the cake from the sides of the pan, then remove the sides. When the cake is completely cool, chill in the refrigerator. Glaze if you wish.

Yield: 10 to 12 servings

GLAZE:

2 cups fresh or thawed blueberries, strawberries, or crushed pineapple

1 cup fruit juice or water

¼ cup honey

1½ tablespoons arrowroot starch or cornstarch dissolved in 3 tablespoons of the fruit juice or water

1 tablespoon lemon juice

In a saucepan, combine all ingredients except the lemon juice. Cook over medium heat, stirring constantly until thickened—about 15 minutes. Stir in the lemon juice and cook for 2 more minutes. Chill.

Yield: 2 cups

16

Lovely Parties (Kosher and Natural)

Is it possible to express your pride and joy on the occasion of a Bar or Bat Mitzvah with a lavish party that does not presage a trip to cavity corners or coronary precipice? Sure it is.

Nobody missed the pastries and kugels drowned in sugar and heavy with fat at the Bat Mitzvah celebrations for the daughters of Dr. and Mrs. Daniel Kinderlehrer. As director of the New England Center for Holistic Medicine in Newbury, Massachusetts, Dr. Kinderlehrer practices preventive medicine, and the many fruit, vegetable, and grain dishes on the menu were calculated to keep the doctor away.

And you can do the same whether your party celebrates a birthday, an anniversary, a bridal shower, or a wedding.

An all-natural celebration does not mean that you have to forego the lovely dishes associated with a *simcha.* You can have your kugels, blintzes, and knishes. You don't have to load them with sugar and fat. Follow the kugel recipes in this book and fulfill your wish for good health with every portion.

Whenever you entertain, provide a dish of mixed dried fruits and watch how your guests flock toward it. Raisins, dates, prunes, apricots, and figs are all good sources of iron, potassium, calcium, fiber, and the important antioxidant beta carotene.

Mixed seeds and nuts make another delicious and highly nutritious dish. Combine sunflower seeds, pumpkin seeds, sesame seeds, walnuts, cashews, and soy nuts with raisins, chopped apricots, or dates in several small attractive bowls and place them in strategic places. This kind of wholesome nosh adds to the conviviality and joy of any occasion.

Fresh fruit makes a beautiful platter, a delight to behold and to nosh. Pineapples, quartered, sliced, and arranged on a platter with cut-up melons, tangerine and orange sections, and strawberries make a wonderful presentation as well.

A bowl of apples and pears makes a nice centerpiece, but very few people will pick up uncut fruit. To encourage fruit-eating, cut up a few apples or pears in uniform slices, sprinkle with lemon or pineapple juice, and arrange them around a little dish of honey.

Hummus with Tahina and Baba Ghanouj are always popular and bring the flavor of Israel to your party. Other healthful dips will provide variety.

Tea and coffee are standard beverages at every social function and should be offered. But also offer a nice variety of herbal teas which have no caffein or tannic acid and which will not disturb one's slumber pattern. Everyone enjoys a delicious cookie to munch on while sipping tea. Provide heavenly Granola Bars, Polynesian Fruit Squares, Cheesecake Squares, or any of the recipes in this chapter. All are designed to build good health—and they taste sinfully good.

Low-Calorie Dips—A Smart Way to Entertain

A great no-hassle way to entertain at an Oneg Shabbat, Saturday evening get-together, bridge or pinochle party, or whenever you want to have a ball with your favorite people, is a dip-and-dessert party. It's less formal than a dinner party and more substantial than a tea.

Whether you gather around the piano, guitar or harmonica or agonize about the terrorists, let the evening begin with a glorious assortment of dips, all prepared ahead so you don't have to miss a single beat of the merriment.

Dips can be light, smooth, crunchy, tangy, mellow, and tantalizing. They should be served with a beautiful assortment of crisp raw vegetables. Don't limit your presentation to the old standby carrots and celery sticks. Try broccoli, cauliflower, zucchini, turnips, sweet potatoes, mushrooms, peppers, stringbeans, and rutabagas.

You can serve dips to delight the most finicky palates and do no violence to your own conscience or to guests' waistlines. Add a jolly note to your presentation by serving some of the dips in hollowed-out green and red peppers. Then invite your guests to consume the "dishes."

Pecan Yogurt Dip

Here, the zippy garlic flavor is enhanced by the pleasant crunch of the pecans.

¼ cup chopped pecans or walnuts
1 clove garlic, mashed
1 tablespoon olive oil
¾ cup plain lowfat yogurt
½ cup diced cucumber
1 teaspoon lemon juice

In a pretty bowl, combine the nuts, garlic, and oil. Add the yogurt, cucumber, and lemon juice. Stir to combine. Chill. Serve with crisp vegetables.

Yield: 1½ cups

Avocado Dip

Use scooped-out avocado shells for serving dishes. Place avocado seeds in the mixture to keep it green until serving time.

2 tablespoons lemon juice
½ cup tofu
2 tablespoons prepared horseradish
2 tablespoons chopped onion
¼ teaspoon chili powder
½ teaspoon paprika
Dash of cayenne pepper
2 ripe avocados, peeled and pitted

In the order listed, place all ingredients in a blender or food processor and whiz until smooth. Chill in a tightly-covered dish.

Yield: approximately 2 cups

HUMMUS WITH TAHINA

Introduce a touch of Israel with a dish of hummus surrounded by whole-wheat pita cut into small triangles for dipping and a large tray of crisp raw vegetables rich in health-promoting antioxidants.

2 cups dried chickpeas (nahit)
Water
1 teaspoon salt-free seasoning
3 large cloves garlic
⅓ cup fresh lemon juice
½ cup tahina (sesame butter)
Paprika and parsley sprigs

Wash the chickpeas under cold water; remove any that are broken or discolored. Place them in a large bowl and add water to cover 2 inches above the beans. Soak for 12 hours or overnight; the beans will triple in size. If the weather is warm, allow them to soak in the refrigerator.

Transfer the beans and the soak water to a large pot, adding the seasoning and enough fresh water to cover completely. Bring to a boil, then reduce the heat; simmer, partially covered, for about 2 hours or until the beans are tender. If necessary, add more boiling water to keep them immersed during the cooking. When the chickpeas are tender, drain but do not discard the liquid.

Reserve about ½ cup of the chickpeas for garnish and purée the rest along with about ½ cup of the reserved liquid, the garlic, and lemon juice. You may use a blender, food processor, or a sieve.

When the mixture is smooth, add the tahina. Add more of the reserved liquid, if necessary, to achieve a spreadable consistency.

Spread the hummus on plates or in flat-bottomed bowls. Garnish with paprika, parsley, and a ring of the reserved cooked chickpeas.

Yield: 16 servings

Baba Ghanouj (Eggplant and Tahina)

Another party dip with an Israeli flavor. It has a cool refreshing taste. Eggplant tends to lower cholesterol levels. I like to serve it at festive functions that feature rich foods.

2 medium-size eggplants
½ cup lemon juice
3 cloves garlic, finely minced
1 teaspoon salt-free seasoning
4 tablespoons tahina (sesame butter)
1 hard-cooked egg
3 tablespoon chopped parsley
¼ cup chopped green onion (scallions)

Bake the eggplants in the oven for about 1 hour, or in the microwave for about 10 minutes on medium. Scoop out the eggplant meat into the food processor or a bowl. Mash the eggplant. Add the lemon juice, garlic, seasoning, and tahina. Mix well. Taste-check for seasoning.

Serve in a pretty glass bowl with the egg sieved over it. Garnish with the parsley and green onion. Serve with whole-wheat pita or fresh vegetables.

Yield: 20 servings

Desserts That Dare to Be Good for You

Expressions of endearment fill the airwaves on happy occasions. Many of them are couched in heart-shaped boxes brimming with tempting chocolate-covered creams and chewy nougatines that can loosen your fillings while providing a sugar and calorie overload. Tell me, is that any way to express your sentiments?

I heartily endorse love and affection and even, believe it or not, the practice of expressing these emotions with an exquisite dessert. It's the side effects I would like to obliterate. Must you pay so dearly for your indulgences? Can't you have one without the other? You sure can.

To express your love and concern in the most meaningful way, provide foods that foster beautiful complexions, good teeth, vim, vigor, vitality, and upbeat dispositions.

Your desserts should be spectacular; delightful to behold, heaven to eat, and like your dips, they should not zap your guests with zillions of calories.

I like to include, with the cut-and-serve desserts, one large platter attractively arranged with several pick-up confections—those for which you need no utensils. Walnut halvah and carob chews make a lovely platter. With the following recipes your party can be a time of continuous gustatory pleasure.

Strudel

APRICOT FILLING:

2 cups dried apricots, soaked in hot water for a few hours or overnight

¼ cup honey

1 whole lemon, grated (pits removed)

1 whole orange, grated (pits removed)

NUT MIXTURE:

1 cup crushed walnuts

½ teaspoon ground cinnamon

1 cup raisins, preferably golden and unsulfured

½ cup cake, cookie, or graham cracker crumbs

½ cup wheat germ

1 cup unsweetened shredded coconut

STRUDEL DOUGH:

1 egg

¼ cup vegetable oil (preferably olive)

6 tablespoons warm water

2 cups whole-wheat pastry flour or unbleached white flour

A little more oil for drizzling over the dough

Ground walnuts (optional)

To prepare the filling, drain the water from the soaked apricots. (It makes a delicious fruit juice.)

In a food processor or blender, purée the soaked apricots, honey, and half the grated lemon and orange. (Or, by hand, chop the apricots fine, then combine with the other ingredients.) Reserve the

This delectable pastry is often reserved for great occasions—weddings, engagement parties, Bar Mitzvahs, and celebrations in honor of outstanding achievements, or having a new baby. But you don't have to wait for a great occasion. Strudel will turn any occasion into a great one.

Strudel dough can be made with whole-wheat pastry flour. It will taste very good but will not be quite so "stretchy" as that made with unbleached white flour. If you choose to use the white, you can compensate for its vitamin and mineral deficiencies by adding wheat germ to the filling, one tablespoon for each cup of flour. Sprinkle it on the rolled and stretched dough.

The filling in this recipe calls for a grated orange and a grated lemon. That means you use the whole fruit, skin and pulp—everything except the seeds. Be sure to thoroughly scrub the fruit before grating.

other half for use with the nut mixture. The apricot mixture makes a great filling, but you can substitute any good quality fruit conserve, preferably unsweetened.

To make the nut mixture, combine the walnuts, cinnamon, raisins, crumbs, wheat germ, coconut, and the reserved grated lemon and orange.

To make the dough, in a medium-size bowl beat the egg. Add the oil and water, then the flour. Knead lightly until the dough is soft. Cover and set in a warm place for 1 hour.

Divide the dough in half. Place one half on a floured tablecloth and roll it out. Pull and stretch gently until the dough is so thin that you can see through it.

After the dough has been stretched, spread the nut mixture over the entire sheet. Drizzle a little oil over all. Spread ¼ of the fruit mixture in a line across one end of the sheet about 3 inches from the edge. Fold this 3-inch edge over the fruit mixture; raise the tablecloth, and let the dough roll over itself to the halfway point. Follow the same procedure with the second piece of dough.

Place the rolls in a pan or on a cookie sheet lined with parchment paper or greased with a little oil. Brush the strudel with a bit of oil and top with the ground nuts if desired. Let stand for about 15 minutes.

Preheat the oven to 350 degrees F.

Slice the strudel diagonally into 1-inch pieces, but do not cut all the way through. Bake for about 45 minutes. When cool, cut all the way through.

Yield: about 20 delicious pieces

Delicious Lowfat Coffeecake

A delightful dessert that will please not only weight-watchers, who will find it hard to believe that this cake has no *added fat, but also the kinder, who will delight in its tantalizing aroma.*

THE BATTER:

2 eggs

¼ cup well-drained apple or pear sauce

⅓ cup honey

¾ cup plain yogurt or buttermilk

1 teaspoon vanilla extract

1½ cups whole-wheat pastry flour

¼ cup soy flour

2 tablespoons lecithin granules

2 tablespoons oat bran

1 teaspoon baking powder

1 teaspoon baking soda

THE TOPPING:

¼ cup honey

1 teaspoon ground cinnamon

½ teaspoon grated orange zest

½ cup chopped walnuts, lightly toasted

Spray a 10-inch tube pan or bundt pan with non-stick baking spray.

In a mixing bowl or food processor, blend together the eggs, apple or pear sauce, honey, yogurt or buttermilk, and vanilla.

In another bowl, combine the flours, lecithin, oat bran, baking powder, and baking soda. Add these dry ingredients to the wet ingredients and blend together.

In a small bowl, combine the topping ingredients.

Pour half the cake batter into the prepared pan. Sprinkle with half the topping. Add the remaining batter and cover with the remaining topping.

Bake in preheated 350-degree F. oven for about 45 minutes or until a cake tester comes out clean. Cool in the pan.

Yield: about 15 slices

NO-FAT COOKIE JAR HERMITS

A very healthy pleasure.

1½ cups whole-wheat pastry flour

¼ cup soy flour

½ cup wheat germ

½ teaspoon baking soda

½ teaspoon each ground cinnamon and grated nutmeg

¼ teaspoon ground cloves

½ cup drained apple or pear sauce

½ cup Sucanat, the sugar cane sweetener

1 egg

¼ cup cold brewed coffee

1 cup raisins

½ cup coarsely chopped walnuts

Combine the flours, wheat germ, baking soda, cinnamon, nutmeg, and cloves. Set aside.

In another bowl or food processor, blend together the apple or pear sauce, the Sucanat, and the egg. Add the dry ingredients a third at a time alternately with the coffee. Stir in the raisins and nuts.

Drop by the rounded teaspoonful about 2 inches apart on cookie sheets lined with parchment paper or sprayed with nonstick cooking spray. Bake for 10 minutes in an oven preheated to 375 degrees F.

Yield: about 24 cookies

Mandelbrodt (Almond Bread)

Crunchy and not too sweet, to many of us mandelbrodt is a comfort food. Whenever we were under the weather, Mom would serve us mandelbrodt and tea. In this recipe, adapted with the help of my daughter, who is a wonderful kosher cook—the natural way, we use some soy flour because soy products tend to reduce the incidence of breast cancer. We also use less fat and less sweetening to further increase the nutritional value.

3 cups whole-wheat pastry flour
3 tablespoons soy flour
1½ teaspoons baking powder
4 eggs
½ cup honey
2 tablespoons olive or canola oil
1 teaspoon vanilla extract
¼ teaspoon almond extract
1 tablespoon ground cinnamon
½ cup chopped almonds

In a bowl, combine the flours and baking powder; set aside. In a separate bowl or food processor, beat the eggs until lemon-colored. Then add the honey, oil, and extracts. Gradually add the flour mixture, then the cinnamon and nuts.

Turn out the dough onto floured waxpaper. With floured hands, shape into two loaves about 3 inches wide and 1 inch high.

Grease two 9-inch loaf pans with nonstick spray. Place a loaf in each and bake in a preheated 350-degree F. oven for about 30 minutes, until a cake tester comes out clean.

While still warm, cut into slices about ½-inch

thick. Place the slices on a cookie sheet and brown them lightly in a hot oven. Watch them carefully, lest they burn.

Yield: 40 slices

Carob Variation: Before you shape the loaves, remove a fourth of the dough and add 3 tablespoons of carob powder to it. Form this piece into a ½-inch roll. Wrap the white dough around it. Shape into 2 rolls and bake.

PUMPKIN CREAM CHEESE ROLL

Pumpkin is a goldmine of beta carotene. What a delightful way to increase your health insurance! Spices enhance the flavor of this delicious cake wrapped around a cream cheese filling that tastes like a zillion calories but is actually a weight-watcher's delight.

THE BATTER:

3 eggs

¾ cup fresh pumpkin, cooked and mashed, or solid-pack canned pumpkin

⅔ cup honey

1 teaspoon lemon juice

¾ cup whole-wheat pastry flour

1 teaspoon baking powder

2 teaspoons ground cinnamon

1 teaspoon ground ginger

½ teaspoon freshly grated nutmeg

1 cup finely chopped nuts (optional)

THE FILLING:

6 ounces reduced-calorie cream cheese, or 3 ounces cottage cheese and 3 ounces cream cheese

2 tablespoons honey

½ teaspoon vanilla extract

½ teaspoon lemon juice

To make the batter, in a bowl or food processor beat the eggs until lemon-colored. Beat in the pumpkin, honey, and lemon juice. Combine the dry ingredients and fold into the pumpkin mixture.

Spread the batter on a jellyroll pan that has been greased or lined with parchment paper. Top with chopped nuts if desired. Bake in a preheated 350-degree F. oven for 15 minutes. Roll up with the parchment paper or, if you didn't use parchment paper, turn onto a dish towel sprinkled with a little flour. Roll up and let the roll cool.

To prepare the filling, combine all of the filling ingredients in a blender or food processor.

When the roll is cool, unroll it and spread with the filling. Roll up again, enclosing the filling. At this point you may refrigerate it, freeze it, or serve it.

Yield: 1 roll, which can be sliced into 10 nice portions

You can have your cake and your good health too when you follow the example of the following recipes and eliminate the fat and substitute an equal amount of applesauce, pear sauce, or prune purée.

BECCA'S APPLESAUCE SPICE CAKE

Here's all the good things baked into one cake without any added fat. Serve it at an Oneg Shabbat. Your friends will bless you.

2 eggs
1 cup honey
3 cups applesauce (divided)
3 cups whole-wheat pastry flour
¼ cup soy flour
¼ cup wheat germ
¼ cup wheat bran
2 tablespoons oat bran
2 tablespoons lecithin granules
2 teaspoons baking soda
1 teaspoon ground cinnamon
½ teaspoon grated nutmeg
1 cup raisins
1 cup chopped walnuts

In a large bowl or food processor, beat the eggs until they are fluffy and lemon-colored. Add the honey and 1 cup of the applesauce.

In another bowl, combine all of the dry ingredients.

Add the dry ingredients alternately with the remaining 2 cups of applesauce to the egg mixture. Stir in the raisins and nuts.

Pour the batter into a greased and lightly floured tube pan and bake in a preheated 325-degree F. oven for 1 hour or until the cake shrinks a little from the sides of the pan and a cake tester comes out clean. Allow the cake to cool in the pan for 30 minutes.

Yield: 1 large tube cake, approximately 20 slices

Ruthie's Hadassah Honey Cake

This fat-free honey cake, developed by the Hadassah Chapter of Pittsburgh, Pennsylvania, is pure indulgence without the guilt.

4 eggs
1 cup honey
1 cup apple or pear sauce
1 teaspoon vanilla extract
3 cups whole-wheat pastry flour
¼ cup soy flour
¼ cup wheat germ
½ teaspoon each ground cinnamon, cloves, and ginger
2 teaspoons baking soda dissolved in 1 cup warm black coffee

In a food processor beat the eggs until light. Continue beating as you drizzle in the honey, then the apple or pear sauce and the vanilla.

In a bowl, combine the flours, wheat germ, and spices. Then alternately add the dry ingredients and the coffee to the wet mixture in the food processor.

Pour the batter into a greased and floured tube pan and place in a preheated 325-degree F. oven for 1 hour or until a cake tester comes out clean.

Yield: 1 large tube cake, approximately 20 slices.

POLYNESIAN FRUIT-AND-NUT SQUARES

Try this treat for the feeling that "I could have danced all night." The fruit sugar provided by the pineapple and orange is quickly absorbed by the blood and carried to the muscle cells, where it plays an energy-giving role.

2 tablespoons olive or canola oil

1 teaspoon vanilla extract

2 eggs

3 tablespoons frozen orange juice concentrate, slightly thawed

3 tablespoons fruit-juice-sweetened strawberry or raspberry preserves

½ cup whole-wheat pastry flour

¼ cup wheat germ

½ cup rolled oats

½ cup chopped walnuts, lightly roasted

¼ cup sliced almonds

¼ cup sunflower seeds, lightly roasted

1 cup unsweetened shredded coconut

1 can (20 ounces) **crushed pineapple with juice**

Preheat the oven to 350 degrees F.

In a food processor or mixing bowl, blend together the oil, vanilla, eggs, orange juice, and preserves. Add the flour, wheat germ, and oats. Process till smooth, then mix in the nuts, seeds, coconut, and pineapple with juice.

Pour the batter into a 9 x 5–inch baking dish lined with parchment paper or oiled or shpritzed with baking spray. Bake for 45 minutes or until golden brown. Cool slightly, then cut into 1½-inch squares.

Yield: 60 squares

Cheesecake Squares

Sinfully good! These disappear so fast, maybe you should double the recipe.

CRUST:

¾ cup whole-wheat pastry flour

2 tablespoons soy flour

2 tablespoons wheat germ

¼ cup unsweetened shredded coconut

¼ cup unsalted butter, softened

½ cup chopped walnuts or pecans

FILLING:

8 ounces cream cheese or ricotta cheese, well drained

¼ cup honey

1 egg

2 tablespoons milk

1 tablespoon lemon juice

½ teaspoon vanilla extract

1 teaspoon grated lemon rind

A few gratings of nutmeg

Preheat the oven to 325 degrees F.

To make the crust: In a bowl, combine the flours, wheat germ, and coconut. Using a pastry blender or 2 knives, cut the butter into the coconut mixture. Add the chopped nuts. Reserve ¾ cup of this mixture for topping. Spread the remaining mixture over the bottom of an 8-inch-square baking dish lined with parchment paper or shpritzed with cooking spray. Bake for 12 to 15 minutes or until firm and a little brown around the edges.

To make the filling: In a food processor, blend together the cheese, honey, egg, milk, lemon juice, and vanilla until smooth and creamy. Mix in the grated rind and nutmeg. Pour the cheese mixture over the baked crust, top with reserved crumbs, and bake for another 30 minutes. Let cool slightly, then cut into 1-inch squares.

Yield: 32 squares

APRICOT-ALMOND GRANOLA BARS

Hippocrates must have been thinking about apricots and almonds when he said, "Let food be your medicine." A half-cup of dried apricots provides iron, B vitamins, and a whopping 7,000 units of vitamin A, which builds immunity and has recently been cited as an anticancer factor.

Almonds, too, are a nutritional miracle high in essential polyunsaturated fatty acids that have been found to lower harmful cholesterol levels.

Incidentally, the almond has been

1¼ cups rolled oats
½ cups sunflower seeds
1 egg, lightly beaten
2 tablespoons honey
½ cup natural peanut butter
¼ cup wheat germ
2 tablespoons dry milk powder
½ teaspoon ground cinnamon
½ cup dried apricots
2 tablespoons raisins
½ cup sliced almonds, lightly roasted

Toast the oats and sunflower seeds on a cookie sheet in a 350-degree F. oven for 5 to 7 minutes or until dry and crisp. Or toast them in the microwave on high for 2 minutes. Set aside.

In a saucepan over low heat, combine the egg, honey, and peanut butter. Stir with a wooden spoon until the ingredients are well combined, then turn off the heat.

Add the toasted oats and seeds, then the wheat germ, milk powder, cinnamon, apricots, and raisins.

Press the mixture into an 8-inch-square dish that has been lined with parchment paper or lightly oiled or shpritzed with baking spray.

Press the toasted almonds over the top of the granola mixture. Cut into 1½-inch squares and refrigerate or freeze.

Yield: 25 squares

prized since biblical days, when it was used both as a food and as a source for oil. Moreover, it is the symbol of the reawakening of the earth each spring.

Carob-Walnut Clusters

A crunchy, nutty celebration treat, rich in strengthening nutrients and reminiscent of that old-time sweet shop flavor.

¼ **cup unsalted butter,** softened
¼ **cup honey**
1 egg
1½ teaspoons vanilla extract
5 tablespoons carob powder
½ **cup whole-wheat pastry flour**
1½ cups coarsely chopped walnuts

In a food processor, blender, or mixing bowl, blend together the butter, honey, egg, and vanilla. Add the carob powder and flour. Process until the ingredients are well combined, then stir in the walnuts.

Preheat the oven to 325 degrees F.

Drop the batter by the teaspoonful onto a cookie sheet lined with parchment paper shpritzed with baking spray. Bake for 15 minutes.

Yield: 36 enticing clusters

Dried Fruit Confection

It is said that King David accepted solar-dried grapes or raisins in payment of taxes. Why not? Besides providing a fantastic symphony of flavors, dried fruits are a good source of protein, vitamins A and C, potassium, magnesium, iron, and calcium.

Figs are champs in the fiber department, both insoluble and soluble. Another happy dividend: there is no cooking involved in the preparation of these naturally sweet confections.

½ cup pitted dates or date nuggets

¼ cup pitted prunes

1 cup raisins

1 cup dried apricots

1 cup figs

1 to 2 tablespoons honey

½ cup sunflower seeds

1 cup natural peanut butter

TOPPINGS: **sesame seeds, chopped nuts, or unsweetened shredded coconut**

Grind the dried fruit in a food grinder or food processor. Add the remaining ingredients except for the toppings. Mix well, then form into small balls and roll in your choice of toppings.

Yield: 36 confections

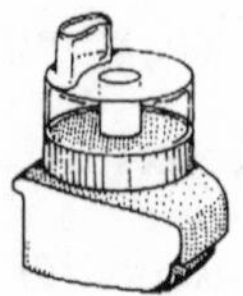

DATE CONFECTION

12 pitted dates

Water or fruit juice to cover

½ cup sunflower seeds

Unsweetened coconut flakes

Soak the dates in a little water or fruit juice for a few hours or overnight, or microcook them on high for 2 minutes.

In blender or food processor, puree the dates with the soak water or juice. Pulverize some sunflower seeds and add enough to the date mixture to make the consistency of dough.

Break off pieces the size of a hickory nut, then roll each one in coconut flakes.

These confections will satisfy that sweet tooth in a healthy way. But heed the advice of one of our sages: "Everything in moderation. Eat nothing to excess, not even dates."

Yield: approximately 15 confections

The date is one of the oldest of cultivated fruits and one of the most important. In biblical times it was used on the battlefield as the equivalent of our K-ration.

Dates provide iron, calcium, lots of potassium, vitamin A, a good supply of niacin, and traces of vitamins B_1 and B_2. Their high natural sugar content makes them an excellent energy food.

17
The Joy of Baking Bread

❧

"Where there is no bread,
There is no Torah."
—Ethics of the Fathers

In that one pithy sentence, the early Jewish sages expressed the philosophy of a brand new concept in health care: holistic medicine, which maintains that to be healthy one must enjoy a harmonious balance of body, mind, and spirit.

If the body is not well nourished, the mind cannot concentrate and the spirit will soon droop. Therefore, where there is no bread (sustenance), there can be no energy for learning, wisdom, and spiritual insights (Torah).

To the sages of old, bread was the generic term for food and sustenance. In those days flour was not refined and doused with chemicals. Bread was indeed the staff of life.

Baking the Sabbath Loaf

I used to love to watch my mother bake challah. There was a special glow about her, her cheeks pink and her eyes full of stars. She sang as she mixed, kneaded, and braided shiny challahs dotted with poppy seeds, sesame seeds, or black caraway (karnitchka). She always made a few small challahs for the eager little mouths that couldn't wait till after Friday night candlelighting for a heavenly taste.

Even more than eating challah, baking it gives wings to the spirit, especially when one observes the practice of "taking challah." This is the age-old practice of taking a small piece of dough (about the size of a walnut), which may be wrapped in foil, and casting it into the oven while whispering a prayer for the welfare of loved ones and for peace in the world. This tradition dates back to the time when loaves were carried to the Priests in the Temple in Jerusalem.

WHEAT AND SOY CHALLAH

This is a highly nutritious Sabbath twist. Two loaves are placed on the Sabbath table to recall the double portion of manna that fell in the desert every Friday.

2 tablespoons active dry yeast or 2 yeast cakes

½ cup lukewarm water

4 eggs

3 tablespoons olive or canola oil

1 tablespoon honey

1 teaspoon salt (optional)

2 cups hot water

4 cups whole-wheat bread flour

½ cup soy flour

3½ cups unbleached white or 3 cups whole-wheat pastry flour

1 cup unbleached white or popcorn flour (To make popcorn flour, pop the corn, blenderize, then strain. Popcorn adds lightness to whole-wheat flour.)

1 teaspoon water

Poppy, sesame, or caraway seeds

Dissolve the yeast in the ½ cup lukewarm water. Beat the eggs and reserve 2 tablespoons to be used for brushing the loaves later.

In a large bowl, combine the oil, honey, salt (if desired), beaten eggs, and hot water. When the mixture cools to a bit hotter than lukewarm, add the yeast mixture. Mix well with a wooden spoon. Gradually add the 4 cups of whole-wheat bread flour, reserving some for the kneading board. Mix well.

Combine the remaining flours and add to the yeast mixture and work it in. Let the dough rest for 10 minutes, then knead the dough on a floured board for about 10 minutes. If the dough is too sticky, add a little more flour. A little oil on your hands makes for easier handling.

Form the dough into a ball and place it in an oiled bowl. Turn to grease all sides. Cover with a slightly damp dishtowel and set in a warm but not hot place for about 2 hours—until it doubles in bulk.

Punch down the dough and knead again for a few minutes. Divide the dough in half and shape each half into a braided loaf.

You braid a challah the same way you do a pigtail: For each challah, divide the dough into three equal sections. Roll each out just a bit longer than the pan in which you will bake the challah. Pinch the strands together at one end, then take the strand on the outer right and cross it over the middle strand; then take the strand on the outer left and cross it over the middle. Repeat this procedure until you have completed shaping the challah. Pinch the strands together at the other end.

After shaping the loaves, place both on a greased baking sheet or in greased bread pans and let them rise until double in bulk—an hour or so—in a warm, not a hot, place.

Add the teaspoon of water to the reserved beaten egg and brush the surfaces of the loaves. Sprinkle with poppy, sesame, or caraway seeds. Bake them in a preheated 400-degree F. oven for 15 minutes. Then reduce the temperature to 350 degrees F. and continue baking for 45 minutes.

Yield: 2 large loaves

Miniature Challahs

After dividing the dough, pinch off a small portion from each section. Braid and shape these the same way as for the large loaves. Let them rise till double in bulk, brush with egg wash, and sprinkle with seeds. Bake on a greased cookie sheet in a 375-degree F. oven for 20 to 30 minutes, depending on size. Makes 2 miniature loaves.

If you have many children to delight, make 1 large loaf and 12 small ones. For the Sabbath, you need 2 unbroken loaves. One can be a miniature challah. Incidentally, they freeze very well.

Bulkalach

Take advantage of the versatility of challah dough. You can make many delicious edibles with it. Try shaping some of it into small round balls. Let them rise till double in bulk, then bake on a greased baking sheet in a 375-degree F. oven for about 20 minutes. Use them as hamburger buns. Make them long and narrow and you have hot dog or karnatzlach rolls.

Pultabulchas

The very name of these fragrant, slightly sweet buns kicks off

Pultabulchas can be made from coffeecake dough or from challah dough. Since you already have your challah dough, remove ⅓ of it after the first rising.

Make a well in the center and add this mixture:

¼ cup honey

1 teaspoon ground cinnamon

1 teaspoon grated orange peel

½ cup raisins

½ cup chopped pecans or walnuts

Additional cinnamon and crushed nuts

Combine the above ingredients and knead them into the dough; then form into small rolls or flatten out egg-size pieces; then fold 2 sides towards the center. Brush with egg wash (1 egg yolk beaten with 1 teaspoon cold water), and top with cinnamon and crushed nuts. Let rise again till they double in bulk. Bake in a 350-degree F. oven for 25 to 35 minutes, depending on the size. Makes approximately 12 pultabulchas.

nostalgic memories of the lovely aromas in my Aunt Nina's kitchen and her urging us to "eat, eat, you need your strength!" Believe me, nobody needed urging to eat the warm cinnamony pultabulchas.

ZEMMEL

When the challah dough is ready to shape, pinch off pieces no larger than a small apple. Knead each piece and form into flat cakes. Press each piece lightly down the middle with the edge of your hand or the back of a knife. This tends to give the zemmel their characteristic shape. Let rise in a warm place until double in bulk. Brush with egg wash (1 egg yolk beaten with 1 teaspoon cold water). Sprinkle with poppy seeds, sesame seeds, or chopped onion. Press down the centers with your fingertips. Bake at 350 degrees F. for 15 to 20 minutes, until the crusts are firm and light brown. Makes about 36 zemmel.

Who doesn't wax nostalgic over these crisp-on-the outside, soft-on-the-inside rolls? Make some from the challah dough.

Baking Challah in a Bread Machine

If you have a bread machine, you can use it to assist in challah baking. Here's how: Set your machine for manual so that it kneads and allows the dough to rise, but doesn't bake. Then remove the dough, braid it and let it rise, apply the egg wash and seeds, then bake.

The bread machine bakes only one loaf at a time. My recipe for Wheat and Soy Challah *(see page 222)* makes 2 loaves. To use this recipe in your machine, cut the ingredients in half and do not dissolve the yeast in the water. Follow your machine's instructions for the order in which to add the ingredients.

WHOLE-WHEAT WALNUT BREAD

This hearty bread enhances every dairy meal and makes wonderful nonmeat sandwiches. The complementary protein pattern of milk, wheat, and nuts makes it especially valuable to vegetarians.

1 tablespoon active dry yeast
¼ cup warm water
2 tablespoons plus 1 teaspoon honey
1 cup buttermilk or lowfat yogurt
1 tablespoon canola or olive oil
¼ teaspoon baking soda
½ cup wheat germ
2 tablespoons carob powder
3 cups whole-wheat flour
1 cup coarsely chopped walnuts

In a large mixing bowl, dissolve the yeast in the warm water. Add 1 teaspoon of honey and stir. Allow the yeast to proof.

Meantime, heat the buttermilk with the remaining honey until just lukewarm. Add to the yeast mixture. Stir in the oil, baking soda, wheat germ, carob, and 1 cup of the flour. Beat for 2 minutes, until smooth. Use your food processor or stir by hand with a wooden spoon. Beat in enough of the remaining flour to make a stiff dough.

Turn out the dough onto a floured surface, and knead until it is smooth and elastic, about 10 minutes, adding only as much flour as needed to keep it from sticking. Place the dough in an oiled bowl, then turn it so that all surfaces are oiled. Cover with wax paper and a clean tea towel. Let rise in a warm place—you could use a heating pad on its lowest setting—until it doubles in bulk, 1 to 1½ hours.

Butter or shpritz with baking spray a 9 x 5–inch loaf pan.

Punch down the dough, turn it out onto a floured surface and knead a few times. Roll into a rectangle approximately 15 x 10 inches. Sprinkle the nuts evenly over the dough. Roll up, starting at the 10-inch side, then pinch the ends together to seal and place the roll, seam side down, in a prepared 9-inch loaf pan. Let rise again until doubled in bulk, about 1 hour.

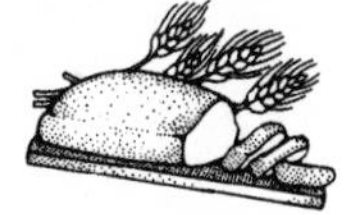

Preheat the oven to 350 degrees F.

Bake for 40 minutes or until the loaf is deliciously golden and sounds hollow when tapped. Remove from the pan to a wire rack. Resist the impulse to chomp on a hunk, and let it cool completely.

Yield: 1 loaf

HEAVENLY BRIOCHES

These French rolls, first cousins to croissants, contribute a touch of class and a heavenly fragrance. Crunchy on the outside, light as a cloud on the inside, they're a breeze to make. They can be stored for as much as a week in the refrigerator or made part way and refrigerated overnight. Then you can have fresh-from-the oven flavor and aroma to grace your breakfast or brunch table without any hassle.

3 to 4 cups unsifted whole-wheat bread flour (not pastry flour)

½ teaspoon salt (optional)

1 tablespoon active dry yeast

½ cup milk

¼ cup water

¼ cup honey

½ cup Healthy Heart Butter *(page 250)*

3 eggs, at room temperature

1 egg yolk

1 egg white, slightly beaten

2 tablespoons sunflower or sesame seeds

If you keep your flour in the freezer, as I do, warm it to room temperature, either by placing it in a conventional oven at 200 degrees F. for 10 to 15 minutes or by microwaving, uncovered, for 30 seconds on full power.

In a large mixing bowl, mix together 1 cup of the warmed flour, the salt if you're using it, and the undissolved yeast.

In a saucepan, combine the milk, water, honey, and butter. Place over low heat until the liquids are very warm (120 degrees to 130 degrees F.). The butter does not have to melt. Add this mixture gradually to the dry ingredients and beat with an electric mixer for 2 minutes at medium speed, scraping the bowl occasionally with a rubber spatula. Add the eggs, extra egg yolk, and ¾ cup of flour. Beat at high speed for 2 minutes, scraping the bowl occasionally. Stir in enough additional flour to make a stiff dough.

Cover the bowl with plastic wrap or a tea towel and let the dough rise in a warm place until more than doubled in bulk—about 2 hours.

Stir the dough down and beat for 2 minutes. Cover tightly with plastic wrap and refrigerate for 2 hours or overnight.

Punch down the dough, then turn it out onto a lightly floured board. Set aside about ¼ of the dough. Cut the larger piece into 24 equal pieces. Form each piece into a small ball and place in large well-greased muffin tins. Cut the small piece into 24 equal parts. Form into small balls.

With a moistened finger, make a deep indention in the center of each large ball. Press a small ball into each indentation. Cover and let rise in a warm place until doubled in bulk, about 45 minutes.

Bake in a preheated 350-degree F. oven for 25 minutes. Remove from the oven and let cool in the tins for 25 minutes. Remove the brioches from the tins and place them on wire racks to cool thoroughly. Wrap tightly in plastic bags and refrigerate for up to 1 week.

To brown the brioches for your breakfast or brunch, place as many as you need in greased muffin tins. Brush them with slightly beaten egg white. Top with sunflower or sesame seeds and bake at 350 degrees F. for 12 minutes or until the brioches are nicely browned. Remove from the muffin tins and cool on wire racks, or serve hot. Any leftover browned brioche can be reheated in the toaster oven.

Yield: 24 miniature brioches

CINNAMON TWIST COFFEECAKE WITH RAISINS AND NUTS

So pretty, you can eat it with your eyes.

3 cups unsifted whole-wheat bread flour (not pastry flour)

½ teaspoon salt (optional)

1 tablespoon active dry yeast

½ cup milk

⅓ cup water

¼ cup honey

2 tablespoons unsalted butter

1 egg

½ cup raisins

1 teaspoon melted butter

½ cup chopped walnuts

2 to 3 tablespoons honey

1 teaspoon ground cinnamon

Warm the flour by placing it in a conventional oven at 200 degrees F. for 15 minutes or by microwaving it, uncovered, for 30 seconds on full power.

In a large mixing bowl, thoroughly mix 1 cup of the flour, the salt if you're using it, and the undissolved yeast.

In a saucepan, combine the milk, water, honey, and 2 tablespoons of butter. Heat over low heat until the liquids are very warm (120 to 130 degrees F.). The butter doesn't have to melt. Gradually add the liquid to dry ingredients and beat with an electric mixer for 2 minutes at medium speed, scraping the bowl occasionally with a rubber spatula. Add the egg and ½ cup flour. Beat at high speed for 2 minutes, scraping the bowl occasionally. Stir in the raisins. Add enough additional flour to make a stiff dough. Turn out onto a lightly floured board; knead until smooth and elastic, about 8 to 10 minutes. Cover with plastic wrap or wax paper, then a tea towel. Let rest for 20 minutes.

Roll out the dough into a 12-inch square. Brush lightly with the melted butter. Combine the walnuts, honey, and cinnamon. Spread half of this mixture down the center third of the square. Fold one third of the dough over the center third. Spread with the remaining walnut mixture. Fold the remaining third of dough over the two layers. Cut into strips about 1 inch wide. Take hold of each end of each strip and twist lightly in opposite directions (like wringing out a face cloth). Seal the ends firmly. Arrange in a greased 9-inch-square pan. Cover loosely with buttered wax paper, then top with plastic wrap.

Refrigerate for 2 to 24 hours.

When ready to bake, remove from refrigerator. Uncover the dough carefully, then let it stand at room temperature for 10 minutes.

Bake for about 20 minutes in an oven preheated to 375 degrees F. Remove from pan and cool on wire rack.

Yield: 1 scrumptious coffeecake, approximately 12 slices

Quick Breads

Super Food by the Loaf

What is the convenience food that goes naturally to school for lunch; to the office for coffeebreaks; into backpacks for nourishment on the trail; into your handbag for morale-boosting sustenance on the bus, train, or plane; makes a lovely hostess gift; and is a delicious answer to that perennial question, "What's to eat, Mom?"

If your answer is nuts, seeds, fruits, eggs, raisins, vegetables, you are not wrong.

The food I have in mind incorporates all of these goodies plus a few others, all baked together into loaves that can be an indulgence of pure joy. Several of these loaves tucked away in your freezer are better than money in the bank. Let the *mishpucha* (family) drop in. Let the hungry children bring their hungry friends. Let the swimmers, the tennis hounds, the joggers, the golfers barge in ready to eat anything that doesn't move. You'll be ready.

ZUCCHINI BREAD

When zucchini overflows the garden and the marketplace, store up its goodness for enjoyment now and next December. Zucchini Bread is moist, delicious, and satisfying. The combination of wheat and soy flours makes it a complete protein. Zucchini is a fairly good source of beta carotene and is ridiculously low in calories.

1½ cups whole-wheat pastry flour
½ cup soy flour
¼ cup wheat germ
¼ cup oat bran
¼ cup wheat bran
2 teaspoons baking powder
½ teaspoon baking soda
1 teaspoon ground cinnamon
½ teaspoon ground allspice
¼ teaspoon ground ginger
⅓ cup chopped walnuts
⅓ cup sunflower seeds
½ cup raisins
½ cup honey
1⅓ cups buttermilk or yogurt
1 egg
3 tablespoons softened unsalted butter or oil
1 cup diced zucchini (unpeeled if tender)

In a large mixing bowl, combine all the dry ingredients. In another bowl combine the honey, buttermilk or yogurt, egg, and butter or oil. Add the liquid to the dry ingredients and mix well. Then stir in the zucchini.

Pour the batter into a greased 9 x 5 x 3–inch loaf pan and bake in a preheated 325-degree F. oven for approximately 1 hour, until a toothpick inserted in the center comes out clean.

Yield: 1 loaf

PEACH BREAD

The best way to store up the luscious goodness of the peach crop is to bake it into peachy breads. Enjoy them now, store some in the freezer, and when the snow falls, you can enjoy again the taste of summer's bounty.

3 cups chopped peaches
3 tablespoons orange juice
½ cup honey
⅓ cup softened unsalted butter or oil
2 eggs, beaten
1 cup whole-wheat pastry flour
1 cup soy flour
1 teaspoon baking powder
½ teaspoon baking soda
⅔ cup rolled oats
½ cup chopped walnuts

In a blender or food processor, puree 1 cup of the peaches with the orange juice. Set aside.

In a large bowl or in food processor, blend the honey with the butter or oil, eggs, and peach puree.

In another bowl, mix together the flours, baking powder, baking soda, oats, and nuts. Add to the liquid mixture with the remaining 2 cups of chopped peaches. Pour the batter into two greased 9 x 5 x 3–inch loaf pans and bake in preheated 350-degree F. oven for 50 to 60 minutes, until a toothpick inserted in the center comes out clean.

Yield: 2 breads

18

ENJOY THE CHOCOLATEY TASTE OF CAROB (It's Better than Chocolate!)

It is said that, at the final reckoning, we shall be called to account for any permitted pleasures we failed to enjoy.

So, let it not be said that you failed to enjoy the many delightful dishes that can be made with carob, the flour of the long flat brown seed pod of the honey locust tree, native to the Mediterranean area.

Many faiths claim a carob connection. Carob is known as Saint John's bread because, according to legend, it sustained John the Baptist in the wilderness. Mohammed's armies called it "kharub," and they, too, relied on it as a survival food. The Romans called it "carobi," and in the British Isles the children call it "locust bread." We Jews call it "bokser" and put the spotlight on it once a year, on Tu B'Shevat, Jewish arbor day.

In ancient times, the seed of the carob was used as a standard by which to measure a carat of gold. As a food which pleases the palate and promotes well-being, carob is indeed worth its weight in gold. Consider what you can do with carob and what it can do for you.

Use carob in any recipe that calls for chocolate or cocoa and you will eliminate negative ingredients and accentuate the positive.

What's Wrong with Chocolate?

Many people—especially children—suffer from nasal congestion, gastric distress, headache, skin disorders, or bronchial asthma and fail to realize that the chocolate they crave is the source of their problems.

This is so because cocoa contains theobromine, a stimulant related to caffein; and cocoa also contains caffein, enough to establish an addictive need. In many children these substances trigger hyperactivity, which seriously impairs their ability to sit still and to learn.

If that's not enough to sever your cocoa connection, consider that chocolate delivers a dose of oxalic acid, which latches onto calcium and ushers it right out of your system. It also binds calcium, causing stones that cause more mischief, sometimes blocking the urinary passage.

Consider, too, that chocolate is high in calories and in fat and low in fiber. In 3½ ounces of bittersweet chocolate, you get 477 calories; in the same amount of carob you get only 180. That same piece of chocolate delivers a whopping 39.7 grams of fat and only 1.8 grams of fiber. Substitute carob and you get only 1.4 grams of fat and 7.7 grams of roughage. This makes carob a close runner-up to the all-time champ, wheat bran, in the fiber department.

Besides being high in calories and fat, chocolate has a bitter flavor which demands more sweetness, and therefore more calories, to counteract it. Carob, with a third of the calories and practically no fat, has a natural sweetness that comes with its own package of vitamins to metabolize it and turn it into energy instead of fat. Furthermore, carob is loaded with minerals, among them calcium, magnesium, potassium, phosphorous, silicon, iron, manganese, and some important trace minerals.

When you make the switch to carob with the following recipes, you will be taking a giant step on the road to better nutrition and more vibrant health.

How to Convert to Carob

If carob is new to your family, take 2 heaping tablespoons of cocoa and mix it with a cup of carob flour. This will provide the old familiar aroma and taste. As carob acceptance grows, gradually reduce the amount of cocoa.

If your favorite chocolate cake calls for cocoa, simply use an equal amount of carob powder. If it calls for chocolate, use three tablespoons of carob powder plus one tablespoon water as a substitute for one square of chocolate.

Since carob is high in natural sugars, use less sweetener when you substitute it for cocoa in candies, cakes, cookies, and pies. In the following recipes, the conversion has already been made.

CAROB CHIP COOKIES

This recipe originally called for a half-cup of butter. I substituted applesauce for the butter. The cookies came out fine, a little more chewy and just a little less crisp than with butter.

If you prefer them more crisp, then do this: after the cookies are baked, put them in a 200-degree F. oven for about a half-hour. You'll double the joy of these cookies when you think of the fat and calories you're going to save!

1 egg
1 cup yogurt
½ cup honey
1 teaspoon vanilla extract
½ cup applesauce
2 cups whole-wheat pastry flour
2 tablespoons soy flour
2 tablespoons dry milk powder
½ cup carob powder
½ teaspoon baking soda
½ cup sweetened carob chips*
¼ cup chopped walnuts

In a large mixing bowl or in a food processor, blend together the egg, yogurt, honey, vanilla, and applesauce.

In another bowl, combine the flours, milk powder, carob powder, and baking soda. Add this mixture to the wet ingredients and mix well. Stir in the carob chips and the walnuts.

Drop by the teaspoonful onto greased or parchment-lined baking sheets. Bake in a preheated 350-degree F. oven for 8 to 10 minutes. Do not overbake. The cookies will harden as they cool.

Yield: about 48 two-inch cookies

**Note:* Carob chips are also available unsweetened. Most people prefer the sweetened. If you find them too sweet, do what I do and use a mix of both.

Walnut-Carob Halvah

A delicious confection rich in calcium and potassium—minerals needed to keep your heart muscle strong.

⅓ **cup tahina** (sesame butter)
¼ **cup honey**
½ **cup unsweetened coconut flakes**
½ **cup wheat germ**
½ **cup sunflower seeds**
3 tablespoons carob powder
½ **teaspoon ground cinnamon**
Crushed walnuts

In a medium-size bowl, combine the tahina and honey. In a seed mill, blender, or food processor, pulverize the coconut, wheat germ, and sunflower seeds. Combine with the tahina-honey mixture. Add the carob and cinnamon and knead the mixture till it resembles a ball of dough.

Separate the dough into 4 portions. Roll each portion into a 1-inch-thick roll. Roll each in crushed walnuts. Wrap each roll in wax paper and refrigerate or freeze. Cut into ¼-inch slices as needed. Makes a lovely edging on a platter of goodies.

Yield: 4 rolls, each 6 inches long. Each roll yields 24 slices.

WALNUT-CAROB COOKIES

A delicious and wholesome version of chocolate nut clusters.

½ cup whole-wheat pastry flour

5 tablespoons carob powder

¼ cup honey

¼ cup unsalted butter, softened

1 egg

1½ teaspoons vanilla extract

1½ cups coarsely chopped walnuts

Combine the flour, carob powder, honey, butter, egg, and vanilla in a large bowl and mix well. Stir in the walnuts.

Drop by the tablespoonful onto a greased cookie sheet. Leave about 1 inch between cookies.

Bake in a preheated 325-degree F. oven for 15 minutes. Cool.

Yield: 24 cookies

CAROB-RAISIN-ALMOND BARK

This is a sure winner! Fast, easy, and scrumptious. Always make doubles.

Nutritionally, almonds are a miracle food—an excellent source of protein, rich in potassium for lowering elevated blood pressure;

1 cup sweetened carob chips *(see note on page 238)*

½ cup whole unblanched almonds

½ cup raisins

Spread an overlapping piece of wax paper over a pie plate. Spread the carob chips in a single layer over the wax paper. Sprinkle the almonds over the carob chips. Place in the microwave on medium for a minute and a half or until the chips are beginning to melt.

Sprinkle with raisins. With the overlapping wax paper, press the almonds and raisins into the softened chips. Press all the chips flat. Place the whole shebang in the freezer for about 15 minutes, until it is frozen solid. Remove from the freezer and break into bite-size pieces. Disappears as if it had been inhaled. Better make another.

and they are an excellent source of essential fatty acids.

Peanut-Carob Clusters

These are easy to make, delicious, and rich in vitamins and minerals essential to soma and psyche.

3 egg whites
¼ cup honey
½ cup natural peanut butter
½ cup carob powder
1 cup whole or halved peanuts

Beat the egg whites until stiff. Mix well with the honey, peanut butter, and carob powder. Add the peanuts. Drop by the spoonful onto greased or parchment-lined cookie sheets. Bake in a preheated 300-degree F. oven for 10 to 12 minutes.

Yield: 32 clusters, each 1½ inches in diameter

CAROB CONFECTIONS

My granchildren call these the "magic candy," because they are allowed to enjoy them freely.

½ cup honey

½ cup natural peanut butter

2 tablespoons hot water

½ cup carob powder

½ cup sesame seeds

½ cup sunflower seeds

2 tablespoons lecithin granules

1 teaspoon vanilla extract

⅓ cup unsweetened shredded coconut or crushed walnuts

In a large bowl, blend together the honey and peanut butter. Add the remaining ingredients except for the coconut or crushed nuts. Shape into 1-inch balls and roll in the coconut or nuts.

Yield: approximately 30 confections

CAROB FROZEN DELIGHTS

The ideal summer treat—cool, refreshing, velvety smooth, and rich in magnesium and potassium, minerals needed to help us cope with the heat.

1 cup milk

½ cup evaporated skim milk

2 tablespoons carob syrup (recipe below)

2 tablespoons powdered milk

2 teaspoons lecithin granules

2 tablespoons tahina (sesame butter)

½ teaspoon vanilla extract

½ teaspoon ground cinnamon

Combine all ingredients in blender or food processor and whiz for 1 minute. Pour into molds, ice cube trays, or paper cups, then freeze. When partially frozen, insert sticks or spoon handles.

Yield: 8 fudgy pops

Carob Syrup

Use this syrup as you would chocolate syrup: 2 teaspoons to a glass of milk, hot or cold.

½ cup honey

½ cup carob powder

1 teaspoon arrowroot starch

1 cup water

1 teaspoon vanilla extract

Combine all ingredients in a saucepan and bring to a boil, stirring continually. Reduce the heat and let simmer for 5 minutes. Let cool. Store in the refrigerator.

Yield: 1 cup

19

MAKE IT YOURSELF AND SAVE A BUNDLE

When there are so many foods on the supermarket shelves seducing us with their ready-made convenience and time-saving promises, making your own almond crunch, fruity-fiber granola, tangy salad dressings, reduced-calorie cream cheese, and polyunsaturated butter might seem like a rejection of the twentieth century. Actually, for those of use who share a deep concern for both a healthy lifestyle and a balanced budget, it's the wave of the future.

Naturally, making your own takes more time than stocking the store-bought varieties. But, when you stop to think about it, what is time for? I can't think of a better use for my time than providing health-building food for myself and my loved ones. There are no richer rewards.

When you make it yourself, you have full control over what goes into it. You can cut the fat, the salt, the sugar, the chemical additives, and those ingredients that may be causing allergic reactions. You can add health-building nutrients and savor the elemental joy you experience when you make from scratch the foods that sustain your family.

You will also delight your sense of economy. Take salad dressing for instance. It takes five minutes to make your own without the propylene glycol, alginate, edta, salt, and sugar you get in most commercial varieties—for less than half the price and for less time than it takes to find it in the supermarket and wait in line to check it out.

Make your own almond crunch granola and you'll never be tempted to skip breakfast or to indulge in the snap, crackle, and plop cereals laden with chemicals and an assortment of sweeteners.

You'll thoroughly enjoy making your own cream cheese because it's so simple and so delicious. You can spread it lavishly in good conscience and in good health. It has only one-third the calories, a mere fraction of the fat, and twice the calcium of the store-bought kind.

You can even make your own baking powder without sodium and without aluminum. There is evidence that ingested aluminum can, over time, accumulate in the brain—causing deterioration and memory loss.

MOM'S HERBAL DRESSING

For starters, try this tangy herbal dressing made with yogurt, which is a boon to your digestive system, and olive oil, now recognized as a boon to your cardiovascular system. It is further enriched with lecithin, a marvelous life-enhancing substance that has been shown to improve memory and actually make one "smarter."

This is my children's favorite salad enhancer.

1 large clove garlic

⅓ cup wine vinegar or lemon juice

⅓ cup plain yogurt

⅓ cup olive oil

1 teaspoon lecithin granules

¼ teaspoon each of dried basil, oregano, thyme, dill, dry mustard, and paprika

Crush the garlic into a salad cruet or a jar with a tight-fitting lid. Add the rest of the ingredients. Cover the container and shake well. Use on green salads.

Yield: 1 cup

RANCH-STYLE BUTTERMILK SALAD DRESSING

A very low-calorie, practically no-fat, refreshing embellishment for your salads.

1 cup lowfat buttermilk

1 teaspoon frozen apple juice concentrate

1 teaspoon lemon juice

1 teaspoon onion flakes

1 teaspoon dried dill weed

Freshly ground pepper and allspice to taste

Blend together all ingredients and the dressing is ready to use.

Yield: 1 cup

GARLIC AND YOGURT SALAD DRESSING

A delightfully tart and tangy salad embellishment. It's low-calorie, fat-free, and can be served over fish, hot vegetables, cottage cheese, or any dairy dish you'd like to jazz up.

⅓ cup plain yogurt

2 to 4 tablespoons lemon juice or wine vinegar, to taste

¼ to ½ teaspoon dry mustard, to taste

½ teaspoon powdered kelp

½ to 1 teaspoon paprika, to taste

1 clove garlic, minced

1 small onion, grated

¼ teaspoon crushed dried basil

With a fork, whip the yogurt to lighten it up, then add the remaining ingredients. Place in the refrigerator for 15 minutes to allow the flavors to meld.

Yield: about ½ cup

MAYONNAISE

No salt, no chemical additives, and half the fat of store-bought. And, I've enriched this mayonnaise with tofu, because soy products have been shown to retard the development of cancer.

1 whole egg or 1 egg white

¼ cup cider vinegar or lemon juice or ⅛ cup of each

1 teaspoon honey

2 teaspoons prepared mustard

Dash of cayenne pepper

Pinch of powdered kelp (optional)

½ cup tofu

½ cup canola or olive oil

Combine all ingredients except the oil in a blender or food processor. Gradually add the oil in a slow continuous stream. Store in a glass jar in the refrigerator. Since homemade mayonnaise has no artificial preservatives, it does not have the keeping qualities of the commercial kind. Try to use it within 2 weeks.

Yield: 1½ cups

FRUITY HIGH-FIBER ALMOND-CRUNCH GRANOLA

Made without any concentrated sweeteners, but it is so flavorful, it will make your tastebuds dance a hora.

½ cup raisins
½ cup chopped dried apricots
1 cup fruit juice
3 cups uncooked rolled oats
½ cup sunflower seeds
½ cup soy grits or flakes (optional)
¼ cup dry milk powder (optional)
½ cup wheat germ
½ cup wheat bran
⅓ cup oat bran
½ cup chopped or sliced almonds (optional)
1 teaspoon ground cinnamon

Soak the raisins and apricots in the fruit juice for several hours or overnight.

Preheat the oven to 250 degrees F. In a large bowl, combine the oats, seeds, soy grits or flakes, milk powder, wheat germ, wheat bran and oat bran, almonds, and cinnamon.

Pour the soaked fruit with juice over the oat mixture and mix to moisten the grains. Spread the mixture on 2 cookie sheets lined with parchment paper or lightly sprayed with nonstick cooking spray.

Bake for an hour or until the mixture is dry and crisp, stirring occasionally. Store in tightly-lidded containers in the refrigerator or freezer. The granola can be used directly from the freezer.

Yield: 2 quarts

Note: If you or any member of your family is allergic to wheat, simply omit the wheat germ and bran. Add more oat bran and some rice polish for extra nutrients, or serve these as optional additions at the table along with the wheat germ and bran for those who are not allergic.

Yogurt Cream Cheese

Put 1 pint of plain yogurt (make sure that the yogurt is gelatin-free) in a colander lined with several layers of cheesecloth. Let it drain into a bowl overnight. In the morning you will have 6 ounces of lovely yogurt cream cheese. The liquid that has drained into the bowl is whey, which can be used in soup or muffin recipes. When spiked with a bit of lemon or lime, it makes a deliciously refreshing and healthful beverage. In the Old Country, fair maidens would add a little rose water to the whey and use it as a facial astringent or shampoo. It has just the right acid mantle.

BAKING POWDER

¼ cup bicarbonate of soda

½ cup cream of tartar

½ cup arrowroot starch

Combine these ingredients thoroughly and store in a jar. Makes 1¼ cups of baking powder. The arrowroot repels moisture, so it keeps well.

To make baking powder for immediate use, combine ¼ teaspoon cream of tartar with ¼ teaspoon bicarbonate of soda. This is the equivalent of 1 teaspoon of commercial baking powder and has 225 milligrams of sodium.

To make sodium-free baking powder, eliminate the sodium bicarbonate and substitute potassium bicarbonate, which is available at some pharmacies.

HEALTHY HEART BUTTER

If you hesitate to use butter because of the saturated fat content, use this creamy concoction. The oil tips the scales in favor of polyunsaturates. The lecithin provides a natural emulsifier that keeps cholesterol in circulation instead of in clots.

½ pound unsalted butter

½ cup safflower oil

½ cup olive oil

1 tablespoon lecithin granules

Cut the butter into slices. Blend with the oils and lecithin granules in a blender, electric mixer, or food processor. Divide into several covered serving dishes. Store one in the refrigerator for immediate use, the others in the freezer for later use. Use as a spread, for sautéing, or for baking.

Yield: approximately 1 pound of butter

20

HAPPY EATING FOR THE ALLERGIC

Some of the most allergenic foods are those that are most frequently included in the daily menu. Gluten, wheat, milk, eggs, citrus, sugar, coffee, tea, corn, and chocolate are just a few.

But don't despair. Even if you are among the fifty million people who suffer food allergies, you can enjoy a wide variety of delicious and nutritious meals.

The minirecipes in this chapter have been devised to bypass one or more of the common allergens, but they also introduce you to some wonderful foods that you can handle with a smile instead of a sniffle.

You can, in addition, follow any recipe in the book by making substitutions based on the guidelines offered here for those with specific intolerances.

GLUTEN INTOLERANCE

Gluten is the protein in wheat that combines with yeast to make bread rise. Barley, oats, rye, and triticale also contain gluten, but in lesser amounts than wheat. Hard wheat has more gluten than the soft wheat from which pastry flour is made. It is important to know that the most nutritious parts of the wheat, the wheat germ and the bran, have no gluten, and you can enjoy them in good health. Other grains that are gluten-free are corn, millet, rice, amaranth, and quinoa.

WHEAT INTOLERANCE

If you are allergic to wheat, you can use other grains, such as barley, rye, millet, rice, oats, amaranth, and buckwheat. Don't be confused by the name buckwheat. It is not related to wheat, not even a second cousin twice removed. Buckwheat is a member of the rhubarb family, and is a very wholesome grain that is rich in rutin, a bioflavonoid that strengthens cartilage. Although spelt is a cousin to wheat, many people who are allergic to wheat can tolerate and enjoy spelt products.

MILK INTOLERANCE

If you are allergic to milk, use herbal tea or fruit juice in recipes calling for milk. Or try these delicious nut milks:

- *Peanut Milk:* Blend together ½ cup of shelled and skinned peanuts with 2 cups of water. Strain. The chunks that remain can be added to granola, baked goods, or noshed on the spot.
- *Almond Milk:* Blend together ½ cup of almonds with 1 to 2 cups of water. Start with a small amount of water, then add more water to achieve the desired consistency.
- *Sesame Milk:* Blend ½ cup of sesame seeds with ½ cup of water, then add another cup of water, more or less depending on the consistency you prefer. Use less water when you want a substitute for cream.
- *Soy Milk:* Combine 1 cup of soy powder with 3 cups of water in a large saucepan. Whisk until well dissolved. Bring to a boil over high heat, stirring constantly. Lower heat and simmer for 3 minutes. Serve hot or cold.

Many people who are lactose-intolerant can handle yogurt. While they lack lactase, the enzyme needed to digest the lactose in the milk, the fermentation process which converts milk to yogurt also converts the lactose to lactic acid.

CORN INTOLERANCE

If you're allergic to corn and a recipe calls for cornstarch, substitute whole-wheat flour, soy flour, brown rice flour, potato starch, or arrowroot starch. Most baking powders include cornstarch. Make your own corn-free baking powder by combining ¼ teaspoon bicarbonate of soda with ½ teaspoon cream of tartar. This is equivalent to 1 teaspoon baking powder. If you are on a strict salt-free diet, use potassium bicarbonate (available at most pharmacies) instead of sodium bicarbonate.

EGG INTOLERANCE

If you're allergic to eggs, it may be just the white that is bothering you. In that case you can still enjoy the yolks.

Ducks' eggs can sometimes be handled by those allergic to hens' eggs.

Whether it's just the albumin or the whole egg you can't handle, remember that commercial egg substitutes are not egg-free. They contain egg whites and nonfat milk solids.

(Make sure you're not given any vaccines produced in eggs. Vaccines for measles, mumps, rubella, and influenza are sometimes made with eggs.)

In baking, you can achieve the emulsifying effect of 1 egg by combining 2 tablespoons of whole-wheat flour, ½ teaspoon oil, ½ teaspoon egg-free baking powder (Royal Baking Powder contains no egg powder), and 2 tablespoons milk, water, or fruit juice. Or substitute 1 mashed banana, 1 tablespoon gelatin, or 1 tablespoon liquid lecithin for the missing egg. To thicken custard, substitute 1 tablespoon cornstarch for 1 egg.

Appendix

CONVERSION TABLES

Liquid Measures

AMERICAN (STANDARD CUP)	METRIC EQUIVALENT
1 cup = ½ pint = 8 fl. oz.	2.37 dl.
1 Tbs. = ½ fl. oz.	1.5 cl.
1 tsp. = ⅙ fl. oz.	0.5 cl.
1 pint = 16 fl. oz.	4.73 dl.
1 quart = 2 pints = 32 fl. oz.	9.46 dl.
BRITISH (STANDARD CUP)	**METRIC EQUIVALENT**
1 cup = ½ pint = 10 fl. oz	2.84 dl.
1 Tbs. = 0.55 fl. oz.	1.7 cl.
1 tsp. = ½ fl. oz.	0.6 cl.
1 pint = 20 fl. oz.	5.7 dl.
1 quart = 2 pints = 40 fl. oz.	1.1 liter

1 cup = 16 tablespoons
1 tablespoon = 3 teaspoons
1.1 quart = 1 liter = 10 deciliters = 100 centilitiers

Solid Measures

AMERICAN/BRITISH	METRIC EQUIVALENT
1 lb. = 16 oz.	453 grams
2.2 lbs.	1000 grams = 1 kilogram
1 oz.	28 grams
3½ oz.	100 grams

Table of Equivalent Amounts

60 drops = 1 teaspoon
a pinch = ⅓ to ½ teaspoon
a speck = less than ⅛ teaspoon
3 teaspoons = 1 tablespoon
2 tablespoons = ⅛ cup
4 tablespoons = ¼ cup
8 tablespoons = ½ cup
12 tablespoons = ¾ cup
16 tablespoons = 1 cup
1 fluid ounce = 2 tablespoons
½ pint = 1 cup
1 pint = 2 cups
2 pints = 1 quart
4 quarts = 1 gallon
1 gill = ½ cup
4 gills = 1 pint
16 ounces = 1 pound
16 fluid ounces = 2 cups
4 cups flour = 1 pound
2 cups ground meat = 1 pound
5 large eggs = 1 cup
8 egg whites = 1 cup
16 egg yolks = 1 cup
1 square butter = 1 tablespoon
2 cups butter = 1 pound
1 pound fresh peas shelled = 1 cup
1 cup uncooked rice = 2 cups cooked
1 cup uncooked macaroni = 2 cups cooked
1 cup uncooked noodles = 1¼ cups cooked
1 large lemon = ½ cup juice
1 medium orange = ½ cup juice
2 cups dates = 1 pound
3 cups dried apricots = 1 pound
2½ cups prunes = 1 pound
2½ cups raisins = 1 pound

1½ pounds apples = 1 quart
3 large bananas = 1 pound
1 cup shortening = ½ pound
1 cup nut meats = 5 ounces
1 pound potatotes = 4 medium-sized potatoes
1 pound tomatoes = 3 medium-sized tomatoes
#303 can = 2 cups
#2 can = 2½ cups
#2½ can = 3½ cups
#10 can = 13 cups

Oven Temperatures

DEGREES FAHRENHEIT		DEGREES CELSIUS
200	extremely low	100
225	very low	110
250	very low	120
275	low	135
300	low	150
325	moderately low	165
350	moderate	175
375	moderately hot	190
400	hot	205
425	hot	220
450	very hot	230
475	very hot	245
500	extremely hot	260
525	extremely hot	275

Boiling point: 212 degrees Fahrenheit
100 degrees Celsius

Temperature Conversion

Fahrenheit subtract 32 and multiply by 5/9 to find Celsius temperature
Celsius multiply by 9/5, then add 32 to find Fahrenheit temperature

INDEX

About the Author

Jane Kinderlehrer, former senior editor of *Prevention* magazine, is the author of the acclaimed *Cooking Kosher The Natural Way, How to Feel Younger Longer, Smart Cookies,* and *Confessions of a Sneaky Organic Cook,* which sold over 500,000 copies. A former president of the Lehigh Valley Writer's Guild, she worked for six years at the *New York Times,* where she ran the Shoppers' Columns. Mrs. Kinderlehrer originated, planned, and chaired the conference on the "The New Nutrition and Institutional Feeding," held at the institute on Man and Science, Rensselaerville, New York. Originally from Fall River, Massachusetts, she now resides in Allentown, Pennsylvania with her husband, Harry. She continues to conduct natural food cooking classes at Coolfont Spa, Berkeley Springs, West Virginia and to address hundreds of groups all over the country to increase awareness of importance of good nutrition.